LEADERSHIP PARADIGMS FOR REMOTE AGILE DEVELOPMENT

HOW TO LEAD YOUR TEAM REMOTELY

Benjamin Jakobus
Pedro Henrique Lobato Sena
Claudio Souza

Apress®

Leadership Paradigms for Remote Agile Development: How To Lead Your Team Remotely

Benjamin Jakobus
Teresópolis, Rio de Janeiro, Brazil

Pedro Henrique Lobato Sena
Joinville, Santa Catarina, Brazil

Claudio Souza
Westport, CT, USA

ISBN-13 (pbk): 978-1-4842-8718-7
https://doi.org/10.1007/978-1-4842-8719-4

ISBN-13 (electronic): 978-1-4842-8719-4

Managing Director, Apress Media LLC: Welmoed Spahr
Acquisitions Editor: Shiva Ramachandran
Development Editor: James Markham
Coordinating Editor: Jessica Vakili

Distributed to the book trade worldwide by Springer Science+Business Media New York, 1 New York Plaza, New York, NY 10004. Phone 1-800-SPRINGER, fax (201) 348-4505, e-mail orders-ny@springer-sbm.com, or visit www.springeronline.com. Apress Media, LLC is a California LLC and the sole member (owner) is Springer Science + Business Media Finance Inc (SSBM Finance Inc). SSBM Finance Inc is a **Delaware** corporation.

For information on translations, please e-mail booktranslations@springernature.com; for reprint, paperback, or audio rights, please e-mail bookpermissions@springernature.com.

Apress titles may be purchased in bulk for academic, corporate, or promotional use. eBook versions and licenses are also available for most titles. For more information, reference our Print and eBook Bulk Sales web page at http://www.apress.com/bulk-sales.

Printed on acid-free paper

Contents

About the Authors

Benjamin Jakobus is a tech lead at a large Fintech company. Over the course of his career, he has worked as a software engineer across a range of industries, from large multinationals to small silicon valley startups. He is the author of *Mastering Bootstrap 4*, published in two editions by Packt Publishing, and occasionally writes and contributes to technical and scientific articles.

He received his M.Sc. in Advanced Computing from Imperial College London, and his B.Sc. in Computer Science from University College Cork. Born in Germany and raised in Ireland, he currently lives in Brazil.

Pedro Henrique Lobato Sena is a Senior Software Engineer with over 15 years of experience, 12 of those working remotely. He created software for a wide range of industries, including shop floor automation, tourism, banking, and ecommerce as well as different types of SaaS (Software as a Service) applications.

He received his degree as "Technologist in Informatics" from FASP in Brazil, where he was born and currently lives.

Claudio Souza is a Software Engineering Leader and Founder with over 25 years of experience, 10 of those in remote organizations.

He started as a software developer in a small consulting company until he became a Staff Engineer in Latin America's largest Newsmedia corps. During his career, he designed and implemented applications currently serving over 600m users.

He's an experienced engineering leader and general manager (GM), having interviewed over 2000 people, hiring and managing over 200, and led over $300M in revenue while directly managing organizations with over 50 people.

He studied computer science at Moacyr Sreder Bastos University in Rio de Janeiro, Brazil, where he was born, and currently lives in Connecticut, United States.

Introduction

It is the long history of humankind (and animal kind, too) that those who learned to collaborate and improvise most effectively have prevailed.

—Charles Darwin

After a collective of over 50 years working as software engineers, we want to have an honest conversation with you, the reader of this book, on why agile software projects and teams fail. Over the course of our careers, we navigated a variety of consulting companies, large corporations such as IBM, mid-sized, aggressive industry leaders such as Shutterstock and AlphaSights, and small, fast-paced startups.

We have contributed code to products in a wide range of industries—from TV networks to online grocery delivery, ecommerce, research laboratories, IoT, online marketplaces, education, and fintech.

But no matter what the industry, product, or team size, the projects that succeeded all had one thing in common: good leaders that hired good professionals, and then gave these professionals the autonomy to do their job.

Similarly, projects that failed were led by people who either lacked the necessary knowledge or the required attitude.

The engineers working on these projects had either (i) free reign and no standards to follow, were exposed to constant power struggles by their colleagues and turned the codebase into a swamp or (ii) were so enshrined in red tape and lack of autonomy that they could not produce.

© Benjamin Jakobus, Pedro Henrique Lobato Sena, Claudio Souza 2022
B. Jakobus et al., *Leadership Paradigms for Remote Agile Development*,
https://doi.org/10.1007/978-1-4842-8719-4_1

As software engineers, we like to tell ourselves that the codebase defines a successful product: clean, easy to understand, testable, well-structured. However, this is only partially true. The main pillar of any product is the people behind it, and the main challenges in software engineering today are human, not technical. A bad codebase can be refactored and made robust by good engineers and a leader who knows how to facilitate it. At the same time, a good codebase can be ruined in a matter of weeks by lack of direction, lack of oversight, and pent-up frustration. The latter not only impacts code, but inevitably leads to wider problems within the team. If not contained by leaders, these problems quickly expand beyond the team. Rot spreads, and once settled in within a company, it can become very difficult to clean up. Like steering a massive oil tanker, fixing dysfunctional teams takes a tremendous amount of time and force, and often entails a heavy cost.

Important Terms to Remember

Before we dive into the details of the above, we should define some terms. Specifically, we should clarify what we mean by successful and unsuccessful products and how we are to understand the term "dysfunctional teams." We will begin with the latter.

Dysfunctional Teams

At one point or another in our careers, we have probably all been part of a team that was dysfunctional. We all "felt" that things were not working as they should be, but what exactly does that entail? From our experience, teams are dysfunctional if the individuals composing the team cannot work together toward achieving a common objective. Similarly, an organization that has a great development team can be considered dysfunctional once those people involved in "achieving the team's mission" are not working in tandem.

In other words, the people composing the company are not building a product/solution together. Instead, any advancement toward the goal requires an inordinate amount of effort.

Team members compete and direct their force and energy against each other rather than channel it toward achieving the objective. Dysfunctional teams leave members emotionally drained and produce output that is of poor quality.

Precise definitions of dysfunctional teams vary, but they tend to converge on "Lencioni's Five Dysfunctions of a Team":[1]

---

[1] "The Five Dysfunctions of a Team: A Leadership Fable" by Patrick Lencioni, ISBN-10: 0787960756

1. **Absence of Trust** – The fear of being vulnerable with team members prevents building trust.

2. **Fear of Conflict** – The desire to preserve artificial harmony stifles the occurrence of productive ideological conflict.

3. **Lack of Commitment** – The lack of clarity of buy-in prevents team members from making decisions they will stick to.

4. **Avoidance of Accountability** – The need to avoid interpersonal discomfort prevents team members from holding one another accountable.

5. **Inattention to Results** – Pursuing individual goals and personal status erodes the focus on collective success.

In contrast, well-functioning teams exhibit the inverse of the above attributes, which means they:

1. Frequently produce high-quality work

2. Maintain a friendly, collaborative environment

3. Use friction and disagreements to their advantage

4. Interact well with other teams

5. Are committed, have a clear hierarchy, and hold members accountable

6. Trusting and attentive

Worded differently, members in well-functioning teams know that they are all in the same boat, understand their role and the impact it has, and thus produce successful products.

Successful and Unsuccessful Products

This leads us to our second definition: What are successful software products? From a bird's eye view, successful products are those that provide value to the user, providing solutions to existing problems while helping a company to achieve its goals.

Creating a successful product does not mean creating a perfect product. Indeed, the most successful products are often far from perfect and require many iterations and generations to reach widespread adoption. However, they solve a problem and do so in a manner that is scalable. Conversely, unsuccessful products are ones that fail to solve a problem—either due to bad quality, because their creators failed to understand the problem that they were trying to solve in the first place, or because they take so long that they become irrelevant by the time they're completed.

Leaders

Last but not least, we need to clarify what we mean when we refer to a leader. Roles across companies often have different meanings. In startups, there might be no engineering manager, and the CTO or founder might implicitly assume the role of principal software engineer, manager, and team lead. In other companies, roles might be better defined, but titles change. Some companies have no team leads but only senior software engineers or managers. Other companies might call tech leads "DRIs" (Directly Responsible Individuals), and their responsibilities might overlap with those of a principal software engineer or team lead.

Then again in other companies, the team lead might assume more of a managerial role. And so on, so forth. Therefore, we want to encompass all of these roles under the umbrella term leader. From our perspective, *a leader is anyone who has the ability to direct other people and influence their decisions, whether they hold a formal title or not.*

A leader is a guiding hand, who can change processes and standards within an organization, and who acts as a facilitator between different stakeholders. Leaders can orchestrate far-reaching change—either through direct decisions or because their decisions have a cascading effect.

With these definitions in place, we can gain a better understanding of the scope of this book, which is concerned with identifying and rectifying the most common mistakes that lead to dysfunctional remote agile teams and hence unsuccessful products.

Pillars at a Glance

Based on our experience, there are nine pillars to successfully lead remote agile teams (Figure 1-1), each of which is discussed in detail in a dedicated chapter.

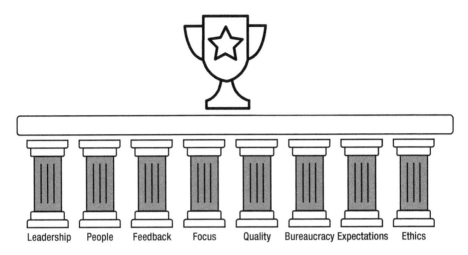

Figure 1-1. Summarizing the nine pillars for successful leadership of remote agile teams

Leadership

The first of these pillars is **leadership and management**. People are the most important asset that a company has. This means that, when looking at the big picture, good people management is generally more critical than good technical management. Being a good leader therefore requires being good at facilitating interactions between people. And this can only be achieved when striking the balance between micromanaging (bad), maintaining presence, and technical oversight (good). At the same time, it involves knowing how and when to shield your team; how to funnel information; how to manage deadlines; and how and when to provide autonomy and calibrate expectations.

People

The second pillar revolves around **hiring the right people**. This requires knowing how to identify good and bad engineers, and understanding what the cost of each incurs. Furthermore, being good at hiring people means understanding and valuing experience. Many times, recruiters focus solemnly on the technical abilities of engineers, neglecting the fact that decisions made by engineers, while technically correct, can fundamentally impact and change the project down the line. Understanding what decisions can be changed later, being exposed to dealing with other people's past decisions as well as navigating "unknown unknowns," is more important than technical knowledge, as the latter can be learned quickly but the former can only be gained over time. Identifying engineers that have lived through their past mistakes, and hence are unlikely to repeat them while working for you, is a crucial skill set when it comes to attracting talent.

Feedback

The third pillar is **feedback**, and involves realizing that feedback is a tool for continuous improvement—both from a personal and organizational perspective. Being "good at feedback" means listening to software engineers (e.g., understanding what is not being said) and acting on the feedback provided (knowing how to identify feedback that helps the team's purpose and communicating this effectively).

Focus

The fourth pillar concerns **focus**. That is, balancing the costs of change and inaction. Setting a goal on Monday and then changing it on Tuesday while expecting great results Wednesday just won't work, and leaders need to understand this. At the same time, the company cannot become a massive oil tanker that is impossible to maneuver. It is important for the product to continuously evolve—one iteration at a time. Products that standstill (due to bureaucracy or inaction) will cause them to eventually disintegrate and fail. Managing these trade-offs between engineering and changes in the product is crucial and raises the question to what degree changes are permissible. The answer is rooted in a quote by Steven Covey: "The main thing is to keep the main thing the main thing." In other words, to succeed one needs to maintain focus and consistency. This also entails understanding the difference between starvation and drowning:

Death through absence or excess. When we starve, we die because we do not have enough of one thing. Drowning, on the other hand, means dying because we have too much of something (in this case water).

Quality

Quality is the fifth pillar and is concerned with how to set high standards for your team. We all tend to sink to our lowest permissible level. If you set low standards, the team will adopt low standards. If you set high standards, your team will try to meet those. At the heart of this notion is the "broken window theory," adopted from criminology.

In short, and adapted to the context of software engineering, it goes like this: When you start working on a poor codebase or join a dysfunctional team, then you won't feel bad for misbehaving or writing further garbage code. However, when you start working on a good codebase or join a high-performing team, then there is a psychological factor that inhibits you from degrading the environment since it would be very easy to link the messy code or snarky comments back to you. You would be "the only guy pooping in the park," so to speak. Therefore, communicating clearly that code quality, usability, and security are priorities is important as this is the expectation that your team will have to meet.

Expectation Management, Bureaucracy Reduction, and Ethics

The last three pillars are equally as important as the first and involve **expectation management, bureaucracy reduction, and ethics**. Focusing on the latter, we have found that weak ethical positions are most often due to the following factors: (i) excessive ego, (ii) lack of empathy, and (iii) a leadership that is excessively obsessed with metrics (which oftentimes they do not fully understand). The latter means that charts become an end in itself, causing people to lose track of what is or isn't ethical. The journey to this stage is always the same: Leaders might initially believe in their product or goal, but then lose themselves by focusing too much on their ego, metrics, and the solution they have (instead of focusing on the problem). Oftentimes, leaders try to aim for good metrics rather than good products. That is, instead of building a good product that then moves the needle, they try to move the needle directly. Moving metrics therefore becomes the goal and is placed above loyalty to the customer. Eventually, this becomes difficult to correct for a company as a whole.

Here Macbeth comes to mind: *"I am in blood / Stepped in so far that should I wade no more, / Returning were as tedious as go o'er."* Applying MacBeth's point of no return to the context of building software products means building a product that is inherently low quality since it is geared at moving some metric (or personal goal), rather than geared at providing value to users. Once this poor product reaches a certain stage, it becomes so difficult to salvage, continuing down the wrong path almost becomes easier than turning around. In order to avoid this trap, leaders should (i) create an environment which minimizes the negative impact of big egos and (ii) ensure that each decision they make allows the company to earn money by providing value; not by driving metrics.

Conclusion

Last but not least, it is important to note that this book is geared toward those who are in, or want to get into, a technical leadership position within the field of software engineering—senior software engineers, startup founders, engineering managers, or team/tech leads. This does not mean that less technical leaders will not find this book interesting (on the contrary: we hope they do). However, it does imply that some of the topics we discuss might not translate higher up the hierarchy (e.g., to the C-Suite level). Indeed, depending on the size of your organization and structure, some aspects of our conversation might apply differently, or might not apply at all. We therefore urge you, the reader, to use your own good judgment on whether the knowledge we share here makes sense for your context. After all, we are trying to have a conversation with you and share our collective experiences. We are not trying to fool you into believing that *"this is all there is to know."* Leading people and building products is difficult and extremely complex, and no one book can teach you all that there is to know. All that a single book can do is teach concepts, change your perspective a little, or awake new thoughts in you. As Franz Kafka famously said: *"A book must be the axe for the frozen sea within us."* We hope that this book serves as such an axe.

Leadership

> *The pessimist complains about the wind. The optimist expects it to change. The leader adjusts the sails.*
>
> —John Maxwell

Leadership, Leaders, leadership teams, our leaders, etc.

In the corporate world, these terms are often used interchangeably with boss or manager; it has become yet another buzzword. Yet, people forget the original meaning of the word leader: "the one who leads." A guide.

It is essential to keep the distinction in mind because of a fundamental difference between bosses and managers: While management can be assigned, **leadership can only be earned**.

As guides, leaders are people who successfully **lead** a group through a path, taking them where they need to be and eliminating, or minimizing, the dangers along the way.

For example: Imagine you're on a safari.

The person in charge is inconsistent, insecure, constantly making bad decisions, and ignores the feedback and advice.

Would you trust this person? Would you go along with them or seek their guidance?

B. Jakobus et al., *Leadership Paradigms for Remote Agile Development*,
https://doi.org/10.1007/978-1-4842-8719-4_2

Imagine that on the same safari, someone else argues against the person in charge and starts giving consistently reasonable suggestions, shows a calmer demeanor, and is often listening to what the rest of the group has to say, using their judgment to make the right call and constructively disagreeing when they think it's right.

Who would you instead **follow**?

Keeping the distinction between leaders and managers in mind is important for several reasons. First and foremost, it is one of the root causes of bad management, because when leadership is confused with management, it creates the impression that people are expected to follow a manager blindly. In reality, these managers still need to put in the work to become leaders and gain their report's trust and respect. This misunderstanding can lead to friction and conflict, and hence lessens a manager's effectiveness. Furthermore, it can also lead to a reduction or lack of ownership which in turn makes delegation harder because, while most teams have one manager, they can have multiple leaders.

For example, in software development teams, it's not uncommon to have people who enjoy and focus more on the tech side and others who focus more on the product side.

While the former is best suited to make technical decisions, the latter likely knows the user better and better influences product directions. Each of these hypothetical people is a leader in their area of expertise, and neither of them needs to be the manager of the team.

Leadership is about guidance and orchestration, not about control. Good managers strive to hire people who are better than them because good managers are also good leaders and, as such, they want the whole team to succeed. This requires relinquishing control and having other people lead when they're best suited, which incidentally helps a manager to scale its impacts and have broader influence in a company.

Management is also a stable role, but leadership can fluctuate over time. When a manager hires someone that's more experienced in an area than they are, they don't stop being managers of that area, but they can stop leading that area by delegating it to this new hire.

There's a popular saying *"People Don't Leave Bad Jobs, They Leave Bad Managers."*

Whenever you hear that, keep in mind that they're not leaving because they have bad managers, they're leaving because they have no leaders and feel like they're going nowhere.

It's also important to keep in mind something that is often forgotten: leadership can be lost.

In the Same Way, That Leadership Can Be Earned; It Can Be Lost

While a manager can be assigned to a group at any given time, the factors keeping them in the role are external and procedural. On the other hand, leadership is defined by a person's ability to influence their followers, and as a consequence, it's much more subjective and fragile.

A company can remove a manager, but any follower can stop feeling someone is their leader, at any given time. This makes the work of maintaining your leadership something vital which requires constant maintenance, as gaining someone's trust takes some time but losing their trust can happen in a heartbeat.

Leadership can be lost in the same way relationships can go south.

Not keeping up with your commitments, not showing the deserved respect to your followers, not being honest with them, or lacking enough transparency are among some of the most basic mistakes a people can make to lose their leadership and some of the easiest to avoid.

If we look back to our analogy of leaders as guides, things that reduce your followers' confidence in the fact you're taking them on the right path and with an acceptable amount of risk are signs that your leadership is dwindling. We cover this in more detail in the "Traits of Effective Leaders" section.

Leaders Can Come from Anywhere

As long as you have people following you, you're a leader.

As a professional working in a group, if you're executing your job well and gathering expertise that your group recognizes as valuable, you are a leader within that group.

Leadership is not defined by your actions but by how people around you perceive them.

Leadership Is Also a Skill

Leadership doesn't have a formal Body of Knowledge[1] (BoK) but can be considered both a research area and a practical skill.

It's something that can be learned, developed, and mastered. Despite being romanticized as something people are "born with," like any talent, it can be fostered and groomed.

---

[1] https://en.wikipedia.org/wiki/Body_of_knowledge

Leadership

There are also many styles. Here are some of the most commonly found:

1. Democratic leadership
2. Autocratic leadership
3. Servant leadership
4. Transformational leadership
5. Transactional leadership

It's important to know this because different situations require different types of leadership. And while everyone has a natural style, an effective leader can adapt to a style that best fits the situation.

As an anecdote, and to highlight how different styles can be applied in different situations, let's compare two easily understandable examples: Democratic and Authoritarian leadership.

People tend to look at those styles from a good vs. bad perspective, but they're not opposites, just different. Each comes with its pros and cons and is a better fit for specific situations.

Let's start with Democratic leadership. People tend to think of it as good leadership because it's one that gives every member of a group a similar voice and gives each opinion similar weight.

It's a style that fosters collaboration and can lead to high productivity and, in some ways, more creativity, but at the same time, it can be bureaucratic, lead to slower decision making, and be more prone to communication failures.

In a normal situation, those pros and cons tend to balance things out, and it's easy to see why it's one of the most adopted leadership styles in the corporate world.

That being said, it's a style that could be extremely risky in situations with a high level of urgency like the ones that are life-threatening, metaphorically or literally speaking.

Let's now take a look at Autocratic leadership.

People tend to skew away from the term. Autocratic, or Authoritarian, leadership evokes the image of a nasty boss telling people what to do and not embracing arguments.

But that's the style firefighters adopt when dealing with emergencies.

When a house is on fire, hesitation can be fatal. Long discussions are harmful because every minute counts.

Do people in charge listen to others? Sometimes. But it's under their discretion to decide what to do.

An example closer to this in the software development field are OnCall issues. Some companies even create "War Rooms"; ad-hoc groups responsible for tackling the issue at hand, with a "commander" responsible for making quick, hard decisions and directing people toward what's believed to be the best solution.

While this is not a sustainable model, it's helpful from time to time and should not be discarded from your leadership toolbox.

The differences between Democratic and Autocratic leaderships work to illustrate how different some styles can be because they are perceived as polar opposites. It also points out the often ignored fact that leadership styles are tools, and effective leaders know many styles and when to use them.

The other styles mentioned before: Servant, Transformational, and Transactional, are other interesting examples.

In Servant leadership, leaders act as if they work for their reports and not the other way around. In the Transformational style, they work through "transforming" followers into agents of change with the goal of changing an entire organization. In Transactional leadership, they work through a reward and punishment system, keeping performance through compliance and the model that describes the military and most outdated big corporations.

This list is by no means extensive, and we invite the reader to learn more about the many styles and know what serves them best.

Traits of Effective Leaders

If the core of leadership is the ability to lead, and have people willingly follow you, the traits of effective leadership follow the same principles.

As leaders work with people, effective leaders are effective because the people they work with trust them enough to follow their guidance, and trust is at the core of good leadership.

Traits

In a work environment, people are expected to do what their managers say, but if they don't trust the person making the request or don't agree with it, they won't do it willingly or won't do it at all.

People have a natural tendency to want to understand what's being asked of them, which is reasonable, but in dynamic environments like the corporate world, not every decision can be discussed. Many times, factors like privacy concerns, regulations, or legal requirements stop people from discussing key aspects of projects.

There are too many variables and nuances that can make the reason behind decisions and requests unclear, which can lead to dissent and disagreement. While these aren't necessarily bad, as disagreement is a normal part of building relationships, a leader whose every decision is questioned won't be able to guide a group toward its goals.

The ability to gain trust built on relationships makes leaders shine. They build strong relationships with their team members, get to know them as people, understand what motivates them, and help team members feel like they're part of a community and not just cogs in a machine.

This way they become more likely to buy into the leader's vision and be willing to work hard to make it a reality.

But how do we build trust? Well, the first step is communicating.

Communication

An effective leader is also a good communicator. They know how to share their vision in a way that inspires others and can clearly articulate their expectations. People are more likely to follow a leader who can communicate effectively than one who can't.

Communication is vital in any relationship, but it's essential in the workplace because it's the bridge that links the leader to followers.

Leaders need to help people understand why a project is important, what people's roles in it are, and articulate what they expect from their team members. If they don't understand what's expected, they're less likely to do it.

People also want to feel like they're part of something bigger than themselves and that their work has meaning. Leaders who can inspire their team members and help them see their role in the bigger picture are more likely to get people to rally behind them. Communication is the way to do this.

When thinking about communication, as humans, we first think of the way we talk or verbal communication, but this is not the only form.

When it comes to communication, there are many different ways to do it. You have verbal communication, non-verbal communication, written communication, visual communication, and listening communication.

All of these are important in the making of an effective leader and they should make their best effort to be good at as many forms as possible.

For example, people tend to think that a good leader is one that's good at telling people what to do, but great leaders also need to be good listeners.

They need to listen to their team members, understand their concerns, and address them in a way that shows they care. If people feel like their voices are being heard, they're more likely to trust and respect their leader.

In turn, this leads to a more cohesive and productive team. And that's what effective leadership is all about.

After communicating effectively, the second step to building trust is accountability.

Accountability

Accountability occurs when one reliably delivers on their commitment. By being consistent, people won't doubt that you'll do what you're saying you're going to do.

Leaders should demonstrate accountability every day and show in their behavior that they can be relied on to achieve results.

If we want accountability from our employees, we must model it as leaders. We can't ask others to do something that we're unwilling to do ourselves.

Being an effective leader requires being accountable for your actions and setting an example for those you lead. When people see that you're reliable and consistent, they'll be more likely to trust you and not break this trust.

By being the example, you start fomenting the same behavior in the rest of your team, and when you consider the broken window effect, you create an environment where everyone can be trusted. It creates a domino effect throughout the organization that can lead to higher performance and results.

When you make people accountable for their actions, you effectively teach them to value their work. Accountability can increase your team members' productivity, skills, and confidence when done right.

It's essential to notice a significant side-effect of accountability, which is simultaneously one of the most critical responsibilities of a leader: enabling an environment of high morale.

Accountability and high morale are tightly coupled with each other. In order to have one, you need the other.

Common mistake companies make is to confuse being nice with not being able to call out when someone is not being accountable. This is a slippery slope for many reasons being of the main ones the loss of morale.

No one likes working in environments where they feel people will just drop the ball and nothing will happen.

Leaders who practice accountability are able to constructively criticize actions without blaming individuals, and this practice will eventually permeate the leader's organization creating a healthier environment where people can disagree without feeling threatened.

In a corporate setting, accountability is crucial in productivity because it eliminates the time and effort you spend on distracting activities and other unproductive behavior and will free your time up for more valuable things.

It's even more important in remote work environments. While bad leaders and companies will fall into a pattern of closely monitoring remote employee activities, tracking what they're doing every minute, and creating policing policies that can feel soul-crushing, effective leaders and their companies focus their energies on building trust and accountability so every employee can be relied upon. The concern around wasted time is not a worry anymore.

What leadership accountability looks like:

- Being reliable and consistent
- Fulfilling commitments
- Modeling the behavior you want to see in others
- Creating a culture of trustworthiness

The notion of leadership accountability is summarized in Figure 2-1.

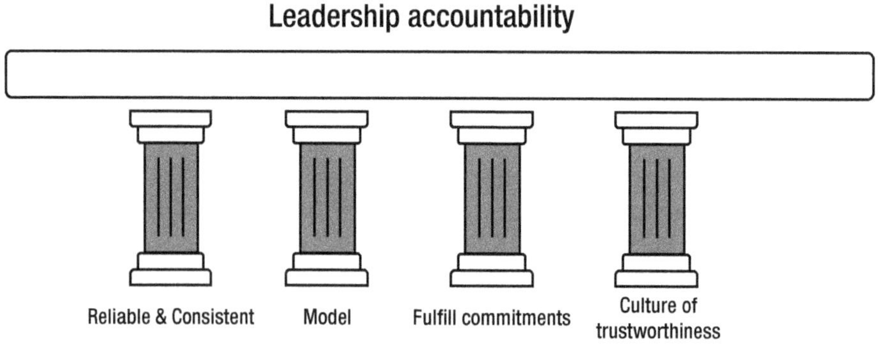

Leadership accountability

Reliable & Consistent   Model   Fulfill commitments   Culture of trustworthiness

Figure 2-1. Leadership accountability summarized

When a leader says, they're going to do something. When faced with new information or receiving feedback and they don't stop to reevaluate their plans this ceases to be accountability and becomes intransigence and can be perceived as high ego—one of the worst enemies of good leaders, which should be open to and good at learning new things and changing their minds.

Ability to Learn and Change Their Minds

It's impossible to know everything.

This sounds like an obvious statement, but people, especially in the corporate world in management positions, often don't act like they know that.

Each person is an island of knowledge—Revealed Knowledge, Rational Knowledge, Intuitive Knowledge, and Empirical Knowledge.

All of which every individual gathers throughout their lives through explicit or implicit means.

Aristotle famously wrote, *"The more you know, the more you realize you don't know."*

This is a phrase that people use, often unconsciously, to demonstrate the Dunning-Kruger effect—a cognitive bias whereby people with lower knowledge in an area tend to overestimate their ability in this area while people with high knowledge tend to underestimate themselves.

Leaders should be aware of what they know, and what they don't and that there's always a chance that they don't really know something they think they do, and the person next to them could have better knowledge.

When hiring a person to work with us, we try as hard as we can to find the best in their fields. We test them exhaustively in as many ways as possible to ensure they're qualified.

So why do so many "bosses" ignore their advice and professional opinion when it doesn't align with theirs?—the answer, while complex, can be boiled down to confusing bosses (managers) with leaders, as we discussed before.

Leaders should understand that they should leverage each follower's specific knowledge to help the group achieve its collective goals. It's part of their job to know what each person's strengths are and how to incorporate every person's expertise into the big picture. While doing so, they'll frequently face new information that often will go against their knowledge and understanding and be persuaded when the situation requires it.

Being adaptable, seeing things from new angles, giving the benefit of the doubt, and changing their beliefs when faced with new learning are traits that simultaneously make a leader more effective and foster trust.

In his book, *Persuadable: How Great Leaders Change Their Minds to Change the World*,[2] the author Al Pittampalli describes how cutting-edge research from cognitive and social psychology shows how a flexible mindset can become a competitive advantage.

In this book, he outlines seven key practices, of which I'd like to highlight these five:

1. Consider the opposite.

2. Update your beliefs incrementally.

3. Kill your darlings.

4. Take the perspective of others.

5. Avoid being too persuadable.

Some of these are self-explanatory, and some take deeper consideration, but they all point to a clear fact: You should rely on your knowledge enough, but not more than on the knowledge of the group.

Or, as the author describes:

Confidence, consistency, and conviction are increasingly becoming liabilities—while humility, inconsistency, and radical open-mindedness are powerful leadership assets.

Trust, Communication, Accountability, and the Ability to Change their minds: All of these traits are essential to a leader, and while they are important on their own, they all have something in common: they're about relationships.

Leaders need to relate with their followers, and they need to connect with the people who lead them, which is far easier said than done.

Relationships are among the hardest things for people to build and maintain. They touch our fears and hopes, insecurities and self-doubts, and force us to take a deep look at ourselves.

Work relationships are no exceptions. After all, most people spend a third of their days with their peers. But the two core traits that help leaders succeed. Traits that are the foundations of the ones previously discussed and are the foundations of effective leadership: Empathy and Courage.

Empathy and Courage

One might question why empathy is important for a leader.

---

[2] Persuadable: How Great Leaders Change Their Minds to Change the World, Pittampalli, ISBN-10 : 0062333895

But before talking about empathy, let's clarify the distinction between empathy and sympathy. Mixing these two is a common mistake and one that is costly for leaders.

Sympathy involves understanding from your perspective. Empathy involves putting yourself in the other person's shoes and understanding WHY they may have these particular feelings. Confusing sympathy with empathy might make you seem judgmental because using your experience as the baseline will lead you to compare things, instead of trying to understand another. Being judgmental is one of the worst flaws in a leader, if people fear what you think of them, why would they follow you? And if they don't, are you still a leader?

Empathy, a key component of emotional intelligence, is a leadership skill that allows you to build trust and rapport, understand what people are really saying and identify their needs, feelings, and critical aspects for leaders to be effective: their motivations, and actions.

Understanding why people act the way they do and what makes them tick will help you guide how you communicate, and how to build trust with a person or a group. It will help you learn from others and keep them accountable while simultaneously increasing morale.

It's a true win-win situation.

With all that being said, empathy is not always easy to exercise. Unfortunately, it's not something that comes naturally to most people, unlike sympathy.

But empathy is a skill, and, as such, it can be learned and improved with practice. Here are a few examples of leadership empathy in action:

- Listen with the intention to understand, not to reply. This means being present and fully engaged with the other person without judgment or agenda.

- Ask questions to clarify what the other person is saying and how they feel about it. Avoid making assumptions!

- Pay attention to non-verbal cues, such as body language and tone of voice. These can be just as important as the words that are spoken.

- Practice mindfulness or being in the moment without judgment. This will help you be more present with others and truly understand their experiences and motivations.

Practicing empathy is possible, but it requires you to take chances. As with most things in life, "you don't know until you try it," and trying empathy means taking chances with other people's feelings, which is understandably scary—and that brings us to courage.

Mark Twain said it best: Courage is not the lack of fear. It is acting in spite of it.

Good leaders have their courage tested all the time. I am not exaggerating.

Here are some, non-extensive examples of the courage leaders need to demonstrate on a regular basis:

- Courage to challenge someone's image of themselves and say that they need to learn more.
- Courage to call out unfairness.
- Courage to expose controversial ideas.
- Courage to admit they don't know something.
- Courage to give someone the benefit of the doubt, even when you feel you'd "do it" in a different way.
- Courage to get out of your comfort zone and try to look through someone else's eyes.
- Courage to admit that they're wrong.
- Courage to send out messages to large audiences that could judge you.
- Courage to say no. A lot. To people "above and below" you. Courage to make hard choices.
- Courage to face the unknown.

Admittedly not all of these examples are specific to leaders, but when people depend on you to succeed, the fears are amplified, and the weight of your actions is multiplied.

And while leaders can come with different levels of experience and have various degrees of success, no one can be a leader without courage.

Conclusion

People who lived through the lifecycle of startups becoming bigger companies shared an experience that is a strange phenomenon.

They often notice that their ability to innovate and pace to build things slows down. There's also a reduced feeling of ownership and impact.

If one stops to think about it, this is a bit nonsensical—having more people, alongside their talents and skills, should lead to a group accomplishing more, right?

Although this cannot be attributed to a single factor, there's a common trend with this growth and a major difference from more established organizations to early-stage startups.

The former has more structure, resources, well-defined roles, and responsibilities.

The latter requires more grit and everyone taking the initiative to get things done.

During the beginning of a company or any project, for that matter, all the traits previously mentioned; trust, communication, accountability, learning and adaptability, empathy and courage—happen naturally.

Every member of the team works hard to motivate each other. They don't want to be the ones to let the ball drop because they care about the people around them and have a sense of shared responsibility.

Everyone wants to feel that they're part of helping something to succeed and want to see themselves as an essential part of it.

In sum, every person is a leader, to some extent.

Keeping the difference between management and leadership in mind can help groups of any stage maintain the same feeling as you get in a startup, with likely the same outcomes.

Management

I believe that every human being endowed with intelligence, memory, and strength of character bears within him a little of the supernatural as well. The highest purpose of the conductor is to release this superhuman potential in every one of his musicians.

—Charles Munch

In this chapter, we will gain a glimpse into the roles and responsibilities of a manager.

Our aim is to present an overview of the bigger picture, illustrating the difference between a manager and a leader. This allows the reader to gain an understanding of what a manager does and an appreciation for some of the challenges they face.

By reading this chapter, we hope that you will recognize just how important the subsequent topics in this book (such as hiring or feedback) are, and how they fit into the big picture. This will allow you to become a good manager of people by recognizing managers for what they are.

© Benjamin Jakobus, Pedro Henrique Lobato Sena, Claudio Souza 2022
B. Jakobus et al., *Leadership Paradigms for Remote Agile Development*,
https://doi.org/10.1007/978-1-4842-8719-4_3

Managers Are Like Conductors

A conductor's role and relationship with their orchestra is a good analogy for a manager and their team (we are not the first to draw this parallel[1, 2]).

Jeremy Cuebas,[3] a Colorado-based conductor, greatly illustrates the role of a conductor. According to him:[4]

*The conductor acts as a **time-beater**, a **teacher**, and **an artistic leader**.*

As a **Time-Beater**, they show the orchestra when to start and how fast to go.

While conducting, they do other things like the meter [measurement], dynamics [relationship], character [growth], or articulation of the music[project management]. Once an orchestra [team] gets started, it can pretty much keep playing even if the conductor decides to walk off the stage.

It's important to understand that an orchestra can play without a conductor. This is especially true for a professional orchestra [experienced team], but even a middle or high school orchestra doesn't need a conductor as long as the music isn't too difficult or complicated.

Once the conductor sets the tempo [standards and processes], the orchestra can mostly continue on by themselves.

If there are changes in tempo, stops, and starts in the music, or if the orchestra accidentally slows down or speeds up, the conductor will need to step in again to fix the tempo.

In the role of **Teachers**, they need to educate the students and are responsible when things go wrong.

Orchestras don't just get together for the first time and play a concert. They have rehearsals first.

To learn new or difficult music, the conductor must act as a teacher. At a higher level, the orchestra is not just playing the music, but actually preparing it for a concert. The conductor will have only a few rehearsals to make sure everything is put together correctly.

Just as a piano student practices to teach their hands how to play a song well, so a conductor "practices" the orchestra to teach them how to play the music well.

---

[1] "Bedtime Stories for Managers" by Henry Mintzberg, https://mintzberg.org/books/bedtime-stories-for-managers

[2] "Manage like a Conductor" by Steven Gambardella, https://stevengambardella.medium.com/manage-like-a-conductor-57a75275ecc2

[3] https://fcsymphony.org/profile/jeremy-cuebas/

[4] https://fcsymphony.org/blog/what-does-a-conductor-do

In the role of **Artistic Leaders**, conductors turn disconnected things into something of beauty.

Through hours of deep and intense study, a conductor will learn the music and make interpretive decisions about how it should be played to create the most sublime experience for the orchestra and the audience.

Each piece of music has nearly infinite decisions that have to be made about it, no matter how simple or complex it is. **The composer always gives us the notes and rhythms**, *and they usually give us the dynamics (changes in volume),* **but many other things are left up to the performers**.

These are the sorts of decisions that a conductor must investigate while preparing to conduct a piece. Then, through words and physical gestures in rehearsal and performance, the conductor communicates their decisions to the orchestra.

Much like painting a picture, the conductor begins with a vision and then executes their craft to make it real. *The orchestra can play without them, but every orchestra member will play it differently.*

Managers and Leaders

At the beginning of the previous chapter, we mentioned that people often use the terms Leader and Manager interchangeably, and while they're different, they're also intimately related.

A good way to start thinking about this relationship is to think about the role of a Leader as an abstraction and the role of a Manager as something concrete, for example:

- A General is a leader in the Military.
- A Conductor is a leader in an Orchestra.
- An Engineering Manager is a leader in a software development organization.

The skills ascribed to leadership are required to be an effective leader. Still, each profession has its own set of necessary skills, which requires that the leadership traits be attuned and specialized to each job—that's what we call managers.

For the rest of this chapter, whenever we mention Managers, we'll talk specifically about the traits required to be a successful Engineering Manager on top of those that make people good leaders.

Management in Practice

There are four Ps in the life of Engineering Managers, and so far, we have discussed three: **People**, **Projects**, and **Processes**.

The fourth and most tangible of them is **Practices**—the actual application of all the other Ps, and the P that Managers are judged by.

As a manager, you use practices to set a baseline for your team; they set the tone for interaction and the dynamics between people, helping them grow, solve problems and conflicts, and achieve their goals. Here, we're going to cover some of the most common practices Managers perform almost daily.

Picking the Right Management Framework

Arguably, the most important tools in a manager's toolbox are their management process.

A common mistake inexperienced managers make is adopting the first management framework they worked with as the standard for running software development teams.

While they might have had a good experience with a particular set of processes, knowing why that set of processes was picked in the first place allows them to adapt.

A good and typical example of this kind of mistake is using SCRUM-like processes for Support or Platform teams. SCRUM, its sprint model, and product-oriented planning processes are designed to work best for Product Development teams, building features iteratively, alongside users and product managers, with somewhat long lifecycles. This context is slightly predictable, and the pace of adjustments and changes is on the scale of days to weeks. Meanwhile, Support and Platform teams' work is dictated by external factors that change much faster than product development, on a scale from hours to days.

In this case, using a Kanban-like model is advisable. Kanban helps balance demands with available capacity. It's a framework that handles well the immediate future and is very flexible to change the mid-term while not too concerned with the long term. Kanban and SCRUM are just two examples of many management frameworks. Still, there are many more out there, and a good manager should be aware of the alternatives and select the one that makes sense to their context.

Many factors can influence the right pick, and here are a few questions you should be asking when trying to decide your pick:

- Are you in a regulated environment like banks or healthcare?
- How many external dependencies, like teams and clients, do you have?
- How much freedom do you have to experiment?
- How much bureaucracy are you subject to?
- How much autonomy does your team have to make decisions?
- How controlled is your budget?

We won't go down the path of exploring the answers and frameworks to each of these questions; know that each one could be best suited to a different set of processes from this non-extensive list:

- Kanban
- Extreme Programming
- Lean
- SAFe
- SCRUM
- Crystal

One last caveat, no matter what framework you pick: don't think you have to follow things to the letter.

One of the core tenants of agile development is ***"people over processes."***

Collaborating with people around you, learning from their feedback, and experimenting can provide great insights that, if carefully applied, can lead you to a process that works to your company, project, and team's peculiarities more than anything you can get out-of-the-box.

Facilitation

Managers bridge gaps and allow people to cooperate under resource-constrained environments, be it time, talent, technical difficulties, etc.

As facilitators, they help to create interactions between people, and when it comes to engineering, one of the most important aspects of facilitation is shielding your team.

In a demanding, high-paced environment that constantly rains demands and questions down upon members of the development team, a good manager acts as a shield, keeping their team out of the rain so they can focus on the tasks at hand.

They act as the team's guardians without imposing their presence—the team knows that the manager is there without feeling their weight on them.

Some instances of facilitation are

- Keeping track of what is being worked on so they're able to communicate the state of things

- Maintaining a pulse on the overall workload of your team, setting a healthy work pace

- To be present at meetings and know how to balance stakeholder requirements with both your team's workload, abilities, and technical needs

- Collecting feedback about the team's and project's performance to drive personal and business improvements

- Finding and negotiating the resources the team needs to succeed

Shielding

Development requires focus. When you pull someone away from their work, you lose the time spent in the actual meeting and momentum. It takes time to pause, switch context, and change tracks to be a productive contributor to a meeting.

It also takes time to focus and settle back into your code. Losing this time can wipe out ideas, thoughts, and motivation. As Ryan Singer wrote:[5] *"Losing the wrong hour can kill a day. Losing a day can kill a week."*

Therefore, you must shield your team from distractions and unnecessary discussions. Although this can sound like another form of facilitation, it goes beyond that, as managers can change processes around them.

- Meetings can become emails.

- Standup updates can be done through Slack.

---

[5] "Shape Up: Stop Running in Circles and Ship Work that Matters" by Ryan Singer

- Support can be done through rotation.
- Tasks can be reprioritized to reduce interruptions.
- Managerial politics and unnecessary meetings can be skipped.
- Tools can be purchased to automate specific tasks.

Managers must understand what should be done, when, and why to make the right decisions to help the team become as productive as possible.

Without barriers, stakeholders will rain requests and demand down upon the team whenever they see fit. Therefore, a good manager almost acts like a border guard: they vet what comes through to the engineers and when.

Vetting requires an intake process to help the team improve interaction across the company: Stakeholders will know what to expect and what they are required to do to get their ideas accepted. Product management will maintain better product oversight since ad-hoc work becomes less likely. And finally, engineers will be less anxious and more able to focus on the tasks.

Lastly, managers sometimes have to shield teammates from each other. Human dynamics are not always perfect, even in the best teams; sometimes, people won't be aligned. Just because two people do not get along does not mean they are bad professionals or bad apples, and sometimes life will lead even the best friends to a clash. They might simply have a personality conflict, and while they might still try to find common ground and work toward the same objective, they will be drained by being forced to interact when their relationship is not at its best.

We all spend more time with our colleagues than anybody else, and having to interact day after day with people we're not on good terms with is tiring and bad for everybody involved.

As a manager, one of your jobs is to help people keep good, civil relations even when their personalities are not a match.

That might mean temporarily reducing exposures while relationships are being repaired, helping people find common ground, or softening the impact via other means.

Overseeing

Oversight does not mean keeping track of the time a team spends in front of a screen or seeing whether they respond to messages in minutes. Nor does it involve installing spyware on people's computers under the guise of "managing their productivity." Instead, oversight means letting people do their jobs *once they have justified their decisions*.

People implementing their ideas without properly vetting them, discussing them with the impacted people, and having a good reason behind them, can pose a danger to the project, team, and company. A few reasons:

- Unjustified decisions may result in problems that can have lasting cascading effects. For example: choosing a certain technology that will be used across the entire project just because you are comfortable with it due to some previous experience, without accounting for whether it is the right tool for the job or not.

- Decisions taken now may be difficult to revert in the future, example: choosing not to add written tests at the beginning of the project can promote code that is harder to test, making it much harder to introduce some tests later.

- A decision may increase complexity, which affects other developers and the quality of the software as a whole.

It is important to note that requiring people to justify their decisions does not imply removing their autonomy to do their work. On the contrary, people should operate under autonomy (more on this later), but not as lone wolves. You do not want a situation where autonomy is used as a trump card to avoid discussions and well-thought-out solutions to the problem under a team's purview. Every good decision should be defendable from its specific standpoint.

Technical Oversight

In order to vet, negotiate, and prioritize technical decisions, managers need to have an in-depth knowledge of the system's current state. The best way to gain this knowledge is to maintain oversight and be part of the evolution of the system your team is building.

Maintaining such oversight can be difficult because:

- Software systems are complex and tend to become more complicated by the day.

- You are not actively writing code daily.

- Whenever weighing priorities, the technical aspect often loses.

While there is no silver bullet to obtaining technical knowledge and translating this into a mental map, the following tips will help you avoid the most common mistakes:

- **Listen during standups.** Managers tend to focus on processes and people, which can lead them to not focus on the technical aspects during standups. Make sure you're following the technical conversations with high attentiveness.

- **Silently participate in code reviews.** Reviewing the code alongside engineers will give you a rough idea of what-is-what and the more granular technical decisions. But be careful not to be overbearing: Depending on your level of technical knowledge, you may or may not have anything useful to contribute or take away ownership that should belong to them. Best leave actual reviewing up to the individual engineers, though. Nothing is worse than a micromanaging manager who comments on code without sufficient technical knowledge. If you comment, make sure you know what you are talking about.

- **Don't fake it.** A common theme in self-help books is *"fake it until you make it."* This might work for some areas, but it won't work when dealing with competent people and will lead you to lose the credibility you need as an effective leader.

- **Keep yourself informed.** If you are unfamiliar with a particular design pattern, concept, or technology used in your project, go out of your way to understand it. Please read up on it, exercise your skills, and build something. You won't be able to contribute effectively if the technology you're discussing is a mystery to you.

- **Don't micromanage.** Managers trying to maintain technical oversight often fall into the trap of trying to do so by micromanaging. Constantly asking people for updates, questioning every decision, or inquiring about why they didn't try X or Y alternatives. This can quickly overburden the team. Even, and especially if the team didn't make the decision you would, you have to accept it unless there's a glaring problem. It is important to understand that managing people often requires you to take a step back and let them do their job.

Keeping a sufficient level of technical knowledge cannot be stressed enough, as this is the key to helping your engineers execute. You only have to be careful to do so, making sure you keep your focus on management and maintaining your team's autonomy.

Autonomy

The word autonomy comes from the Greek word *"autonomía,"* meaning *"freedom to use its own laws, independence,"* and this is exactly what autonomy is. That is, being able to execute independently but responsibly, without needing constant approval and reassurance that you are acting within a given framework. One of the quickest ways to kill a project, or an entire company, is via "death by committee." If every minute decision needs to be discussed by the team or needs various stamps of approval by superiors, then your product will go nowhere. Hire the right people and let them do their job. And once these people can justify major decisions, technical or otherwise, they should be given the space and freedom to execute.

Failing to give people the necessary autonomy has several negative impacts on a manager and their teams' success:

- It'll consume most of their time, as they'll have to oversee everything around them constantly.

- Along the same lines, it will stop them from scaling their impact, which will hold their careers back.

- It also kills motivation, which leads to frustration and eventually people quitting.

Autonomy is critical in remote teams. With limited face-to-face time, and the challenges posed by remote communication, the best way for a manager to ensure a team is making progress is to allow people autonomy and the sense of pride that comes with it.

Good managers use their oversight to build and maintain autonomy within their reports, a notion that's best summarized by a popular management quote often attributed to Jack Welch (CEO of General Motors): *"Communicate your ideas, distribute resources, and get out of the way."*

Managing Deadlines

There are two types of deadlines: **soft deadlines**, those that can be negotiated, and **hard deadlines**, those that cannot.

Hard deadlines arise due to circumstances outside the team's or company's control—for example, a new Tax and Reporting feature is required due to new IRS guidelines and is required by a certain date to avoid fines.

Soft deadlines, on the other hand, are those set internally and, as such, should be defined with team participation.

Estimating how long a task takes is technical and should not be done without understanding the variables that affect such output. Soft deadlines are helpful for three reasons:

1. They help us to align other workloads and plans.

2. They give the team direction and a sense of priority.

3. They help hold us accountable.

A big mistake inexperienced managers make is confounding soft with hard deadlines.

That is, *they treat soft deadlines as hard deadlines* as a way to "motivate" engineers to achieve more. They set deadlines in stone to increase output without needing them to be set in stone. However, all that this does is create unnecessary pressure, and when scope and time can't be changed, the cost comes in the form of poor quality software and technical debt.

The inverse can also be true; another common mistake is treating hard deadlines as soft. Not communicating the expectations correctly and not doing more aggressive prioritization can lead to an exponential increase in pressure toward the end date.

Project Management

One of the core expectations of Engineering Management is being able to manage projects and the features that come with them, which heavily impacts managing the team itself. For one, the nature of your work will determine the skills the team will need, the pace of work, expectations across stakeholders, and so on.

Managing a project requires you to work as an interface between engineering and the rest of the business. Without facilitating the exchange between ideas and requirements with the business' needs, you will not be able to manage a team effectively.

It is important to highlight that Project Management is its own discipline, with an extensive Body of Knowledge (BoK), and is very complex, a complexity that is increased further depending on the nature of the challenges. It is also important to note that most big and small companies don't recognize this complexity and don't prepare, screen for, or train people to succeed in this role.

There are an uncountable number of books about project management, and its nuances are beyond the scope of this book. Still, we're now going to try to give you a glimpse into its expectations for an Engineering Manager (EM) when working in an organization building products for consumers.

Isn't Project Management the Role of a Product Manager?

At first glance, it might look as if project management is the role of the Product Manager. Indeed, some companies do require the product managers (PMs) to assume this responsibility. Regardless, EMs and PMs should always closely collaborate, but the management of the project itself usually is the job of the EM, due to several reasons:

- While PMs have a deeper understanding of the product, the business, the product vision, and the users, the EMs have deeper technical knowledge.

- As the people responsible for building the software, the EM is much more intimately involved with the technical aspects of the product's user experience.

- The EM tends to have much greater visibility into the granularity around execution.

- There's no clear industry standard around the role of EMs and PMs and where their responsibilities and boundaries lie.

When an EM does not understand how to manage a project, the end result is simple but impactful: *The team will end up building the wrong thing the wrong way.*

Building the wrong feature or project for extended periods can lead to a waste of time and money at best, and bankruptcy at worst.

Either way, this will lead to the team's dissatisfaction. In the end, people want to feel that what they do matters. Building the wrong thing is a concrete, even if indirect, statement that all the effort and passion put into their work was for nothing, which can make their manager's life hard to nigh impossible.

Building the Right Thing

In order to successfully manage a project, one needs to understand the potential impact projects and features will have on the business and its customers and, among other areas, this requires:

- An understanding of your company's business model, strategies, and plans

- Domain and technical knowledge of the business and its industry

- A Bird's Eye view of what's going in on in the company, especially if you have internal dependencies

- Identifying and mitigating risks
- Stakeholder management
- Understanding who your users are and what they value

All these topics are relevant and equally impactful. Still, the last point (understanding who your users are and what they value) is where most managers fall short due to two factors:

1. Being too technical and focusing more on the solution (technology) rather than the problem

2. Being too hypothetical, and trying to picture solutions instead of being grounded in how and why users use the product

What is valuable to the customers is not always helpful to the business—not aligning the two perspectives amounts to rowing against the tide. *Remember the maxim*: No plan survives contact with the enemy.

In the same way, having the people you're trying to help tell you, directly or not, that a feature truly addresses their needs is the only way to be sure you're building what matters (incidentally, also the name of a great book on the topic[6]).

Consequently, listening to the users is the first step in building the right thing, which can be done in many ways. This responsibility is usually primarily assumed by the PM, and then communicated with the EM and the rest of the team. Regardless of who does the "listening" at your organization, it may involve:

- **Surveys** – From Net Promoter Score (NPS, a way of gauging customer satisfaction) to targeted surveys around a specific topic

- **Interviews** – Structured, with a script trying to dig for more information, to unstructured like blind usability tests

- **A/B tests** – Building variations of the same thing to see what performs best in real life

Regardless of whether performed by the EM or PM, it is critical to identify and filter out features that serve the user (and hence add value to the product itself).

---

[6] "Build What Matters: Delivering Key Outcomes with Vision-Led Product Management", ISBN 978-1544516189

A company's mission can be changed, reformed, and adapted. However, the same cannot be said about your customers. Once your product no longer provides value to the customer, your product and business will fail.

Managers have a responsibility toward their teams, peers, and the company to ensure the focus on what's valuable at the time and be constantly reviewing the context so they can adapt when things change.

Planning and Prioritization

An unintuitive but crucial aspect of project management is managing complexity. All but the smallest projects (one person, one day) are webs of interdependent relationships of many factors—teams, users, processes, technologies, strategies, opinions, etc.

To successfully run a project, managers need to see the forest for the trees while not losing sight of each twig.

The way to do that without losing control of the project is by creating a cadence of execution where each step takes you closer to the goal by carefully choosing what step is foundational to the next. This is what we call prioritizing.

Prioritization is the art of balancing out your project's **5W2H** dimensions:[7] **What**, **Why**, **Where**, **When**, **Who**, **How**, and **How** much. A method applicable to almost any aspect of a project, from strategy to execution and epics to tasks, understanding how 5W2H works requires some examples that illustrate their many variations and implications:

- **What**? What needs to be done—what's the scope?

- **Why**? Why does it have to be done—what are the motivations and impacts?

- **Where**? Where will it live—where in the system, and how does the user get there?

- **When**? When will it be done—do we have what we need by the time we start it?

- **Who**? Who's going to do it? Who is going to be affected? Who's going to approve?

- **How**? How will it be done? Tools, tech, processes?

- **How much**? How much will it cost to make? How many resources will it consume?

---

[7] Interestingly, the origin of the 5W2H can be traced back to ancient Greece. Hermagoras of Temnos is often cited as first identifying the 5Ws.

If you're committed to building the right thing and are listening to the users, you're already getting much of the information necessary to answer these questions. Your relationship with the internal stakeholders should provide the rest, and you can start prioritizing.

Sounds complicated? It's not when done right.

Planning and Prioritization in Most Companies

Let's discuss what project planning typically looks like in software development.

If you're already working in the field, you likely saw some of this in action—they're rituals and artifacts commonly referred to as sprints, backlogs, grooming, epics, stories, or any variation of these.

A typical way companies run projects goes like this: After deciding on the goals, people sit down to break the work down into milestones, called Epics, hoping each epic will get you closer to the project's goal.

Then they discuss each epic, break it into components called Stories, and select which stories will go into the epic.

With the list of stories, they go through an estimation session and discuss each story, write specs, and do planning-poker or other types of estimation.

With all the stories estimated, they use the team's velocity, a measure of how much progress a team can make in a fixed period, to estimate how long the project will take.

In the end, they hope to know, among other things, how long the project will take, who needs to be involved, what the product will look like, and how it will impact the company's objective.

There are many problems with this process, and they often stem from companies and managers failing to acknowledge the inherent complexity of projects of any meaningful size—as discussed, almost all of them.

Trying to plan out an entire project upfront is an exercise in futility, often better served to soothe concerns, and rarely works to make it successful.

Here's a non-extensive list of themes and issues with this standard way of planning:

You Can't Predict the Future

There are too many variables we can't control that can significantly impact a project.

A key person might leave the company or team, or a new one might join. A critical technology, like an external API, might change without notice. A government, or even your company, can create or change policies.

Everyday one is incorporating new information and learnings arising during execution.

Opinions may also change during the project's life, and the assumptions based on them can mean that a small or big part of the original plan can, too, often have a ripple effect.

Even a pandemic can happen. One can only imagine how many projects were changed or canceled because of that.

Our Brains Are Limited

Society, and the corporate world, often push us to play smart. The truth is that our brains have limited capacity.

Even when working together, there's a limit to what we can see, especially when the web of complexity is weaved so widely, as in the case of project management. Trying to grasp all the parts of an entire project and create an entire map (roadmap) upfront is virtually impossible due to these limitations.

Myriads of neurological research describe our minds' boundaries and how it affects our perception of the world. Still, a particular set of these limits are more prominent when planning projects: **biases**.

Bias happens when there's disproportionate weight in favor of or against an idea, thing, or person. One can have a bias all their life or learn new ones at any point. We often perceive them more quickly when they're against an individual, group, or belief, but people can also have a bias toward ideas and attitudes. Those are harder to spot and arguably most impactful when collaborating to build things.

Let's look at one of the most common: **confirmation bias**. Simply put, we look for, interpret, and favor things we already believe in or value. When facing a choice and presented with two sets of information, one aligned with our thinking and one that does not, most people pick the former without even thinking about the latter.

A classic example in software engineering is when a backend and a frontend developer discuss implementing a feature. Assuming that that feature could be done using either expertise, it's unlikely they'll even consider the other person's perspective. At least when deciding in isolation.

In essence, confirmation bias tells us that *"if all you have is a hammer, everything looks like a nail."*[8]

This biased behavior can lead to many issues in a project:

- People can fail to discuss the trade-offs.
- Blindspots.
- Making strategic decisions without proper vetting.

And many, many more.

The list of biases and their impacts is extensive and beyond the scope of this book, but here are a few more often seen in project planning.

Anchoring Bias

This bias describes how the first fact we're exposed to influences (or anchors) our subsequent decisions.[9]

For example, if you tell a group that 90% of users liked feature A and ask them the percentage that will like similar feature B, each person will answer with a number close to 90%.

If you tell them that only 10% liked feature A and ask the same question, they'll give you a number closer to 10%.

Availability Heuristic

This is the notion that the first thing that comes to a person's mind when evaluating a specific topic, concept, or decision is the right one.[10]

Bandwagon Effect

The adoption of behaviors, or the making of decisions, because a group behaves in a certain way.[11]

---

[8] Abraham H. Maslow (1966). The Psychology of Science. p. 15. ISBN 978-0976040231

[9] Tversky, A., Kahneman, D. Advances in prospect theory: Cumulative representation of uncertainty. J Risk Uncertainty 5, 297–323 (1992). https://doi.org/10.1007/BF00122574

[10] www.oxfordreference.com/view/10.1093/oi/authority.20110803095436724

[11] Kiss, Áron; Simonovits, Gábor (2014). "Identifying the bandwagon effect in two-round elections". Public Choice. 160 (3/4): 327–344. doi:10.1007/s11127-013-0146-y. JSTOR 24507550

Choice-Supportive Bias

The tendency to think the decisions we made are the right ones and the ones we didn't are the wrong ones.[12] For example, if a person chooses option A instead of B, they will likely ignore or downplay option A's faults while amplifying the bad aspects and drawbacks to option B.

We invite the reader to learn more about biases, and we can humbly say you'll become a better professional if you do.

Communication Is Inherently Fraught

People tend to think of communication as something trivial as it's something we do all the time, and while casual communication can be easy, corporate communication can become rather complex.

When communicating with stakeholders, peers, or even within our teams, our human tendency is to assume things. This is the consequence of our many biases.

This is not out of malice; it's just a consequence of our complex biologies, social norms, and psych. We rarely think about these things, but they permeate how we address the world outside. A meeting after a good night of sleep can go wildly different than if you had a bad one.

Other factors, like the volume of information we have to process and our level of attachment to certain decisions, can severely impact what we say and hear.

Trying to capture and communicate all project steps in the first go maximizes all the issues we have with communications. At the same time, this is too much to digest in a short period (relative to the size of the project) and not enough time to digest all the complexities of a project.

Another important fact to consider is the practice of capturing all the communication in written form. We do that to manage complexity and align expectations around what we're trying to do, but we forget this is inherently flawed. Let's see why by looking at a trivial example of a feature called "User selects state for tax purpose":

---

[12] Mather, M.; Johnson, M.K. (2000). "Choice-supportive source monitoring: Do our decisions seem better to us as we age?" (PDF). Psychology and Aging. 15 (4): 596–606. doi:10.1037/0882-7974.15.4.596

TITLE: USER SELECTS STATE FOR TAX PURPOSE.

As a US Citizen, I want to select my state of residency in a dropdown when buying a product so that I pay the correct taxes.

- This is mandatory

- Taxes are applied according to the selected option.

This "User Story" follows the "As a [persona], I [want to], [so that]" with the intent to describe who's going to be impacted by this feature (persona), what needs to be done, and why this is important for them. It also contains a list of "Acceptance Criteria" or a list of items you need to check to validate if a story can be considered done.

Although they can vary in format and content, software development often happens through building a series of these user stories where each unit and increment leads to a finished product.

There are many problems with capturing dozens or hundreds (sometimes thousands) of these stories upfront, coming up with a "list of requirements," and expecting it to be a reliable roadmap to build something.

Let's highlight a few of these issues using the "User selects state for tax purpose" story as a reference (Figure 3-1):

Figure 3-1. The "User selects state for tax purpose" story

Limited Perspective

By definition, the scope of a story will be limited by the knowledge and bias of the people involved in defining said scope.

In this story, the expectation could easily be set to use the 50 US states, but what about the US territories, of which there are 14? If the story targets the "US citizen" persona, those territories should also be considered as each has an equivalent of a state tax. What about federal taxes? Should these stories also account for them, as some territories fall into different regulations?

What about the seven US states that don't have taxes? Should we hide these states? Should we set zero taxes? What about US citizens living abroad?

This is a simple feature with some relatively obvious edge cases. Still, it's easy to see many possible permutations and edge cases arising from people.

One could argue that each of these cases could be captured on its own story, and it's a failure of the people responsible for "capturing the specs" not to have taken one, or many, of these cases into account. In reality, even for the smallest of features, there is a small set of views and insights a group can come up with, no matter how varied and smart they are.

Incidentally, this combinatorial explosion, the rapid growth of complexity due to the multiple combinations of all the variables in a problem, is why projects often go over time and budget.

Focusing on the Solution, Not the Problem

Another common issue with capturing specs with texts is the inclination to define what needs to be done instead of what we're trying to solve.

Our example states that we need to provide a dropdown to the user so they can select their state, but the core problem we're trying to address is having the user pay the correct taxes based on where they live. When developers receive that story, they won't stop to think about the edge cases we discussed; they focus on doing what they've been asked to do.

What if, instead of the original text we proposed, the story had a more succinct description like *"As a US Citizen, I want to pay the due taxes based on where I live?"*

This approach is an improvement on the original story. Because we're not providing developers with a set of things to do, they would be forced to think through the problem.

They would have to talk to stakeholders and understand what the problem entails at the same time of development, which would lead to them having to deal with fresh information (more on that soon). They'd have to use the PM as a knowledge base and lean on their expertise while also developing critical thinking and expertise of their own on the domain they're working on.

This would also give the problem (story) extra pairs of eyes and give developers a higher degree of freedom, accountability, and pride due to being responsible for deciding what to do. In this example, they could use a third-party service to [automagically] get the user tax based on their geolocation and have all the corner cases addressed by a specialized service.

One of the main reasons people don't take this stance when creating stories is because the trade-off is losing the **imaginary predictability** people think they get by upfront planning everything.

Our intuition makes us falsely believe that if we break down some work in all its constituent units, we can estimate how long the work will take by adding up each unit's cost and effort.

As we can see from some previous points, this is futile for all but the smallest of projects.

Static Views of a Dynamic World

Let's ignore all the complexities of projects and their myriads of interconnected relationships. Let's also dream up a perfect team capable of writing the best, most cohesive, brilliant stories.

Would this allow this hypothetical team to plan and correctly estimate a project upfront? Unlikely.

Planning an entire project that can last many months is akin to taking a snapshot of what's known about the project at the beginning of it at a fixed point in time. Even smaller chunks of work (milestones) suffer from the same problem.

One reason for that is that life is dynamic, not static. Things change—all the time.

What if a new tech, that could make a feature easier, comes up? Would you stick to the plan instead of considering it? What if a critical stakeholder leaves your project? What if a competitor comes up with the same feature making the current strategy irrelevant?

Too many factors change every day. Some small and some big, but all affect the project and change its scope in meaningful ways.

A Brief History of Software Development

So, should we stop planning projects altogether? Should we stop writing specifications and requirements? Is every problem too complex to handle? Should we throw away all the norms?

Well, not quite. As we're about to see, all these processes have their merit, and to better appreciate it and understand when and why they sometimes fail, it's good to understand where they come from and how they evolved.

First, let's take a step back and recognize that Project Management is a highly developed discipline. It became a formal discipline barely over a hundred years ago when Frederick Winslow Taylor published his seminal work *The Principles of Scientific Management*.[13] It has been instrumental in bringing forth our modern world ever since.

Taylor's focus was to improve manual-labor-based production and resource management. Eventually, it inspired the rise of new sets of processes responsible for managing increasingly complex projects, like taking people to the moon.

---

[13] "The Principles of Scientific Management" by Frederick Winslow Taylor https:// archive.org/details/principlesofscie00taylrich/page/n5/mode/2up?view=theater

Today, anything from cars to computers to MRI machines is conceptualized and brought to reality using management principles derived from that, which are not unlike the one described in the previous section.

It's safe to say that every product produced at scale these days had a successful project behind them. Some of them even became famous on their own, such as the one leading to iPhone's creation: *Project Purple*—look it up.

The range of Software Development Life Cycle (SDLC) processes we have today is an adaptation of the methodologies developed over decades to build everyday products. In the same fashion, SLDC projects have been evolving too.

In the Beginning

The first SDLC methodologies reflected Henry Ford's 1913 world-changing innovation—the moving assembly line, which was inspired by Taylor's scientific management theory and had his direct support after Ford hired him as a consultant.

In short, a simplified version of the assembly line process goes like this:

- With *the car's design* on paper and *necessary resources ready, the exact sequence* the car will be assembled is planned.

- Then, a person *starts working* on a part and, after they finished, *they move it to the next step in the line*, and handle it to next person, so they can *build the next part by integrating it* with the previous one.

- *This continues* with *all* the planned steps until the car is done.

- The car is then *quality controlled*, and it's deemed *ready to be sold* if no problem is found.

Knowing upfront what to do, having a defined set of measurable steps, and making the workers pure executors of what the managers decided were some of the crucial factors that made the assembly line so effective in cutting production costs, which led to cars' price reduction and making it affordable to the masses.

It's also important to notice that these were big improvements over the lack of established processes in that era, but they came with obvious drawbacks like, ironically, turning workers into "replaceable cogs."

The assembly line parallel in the software development world is known as waterfall development. It was developed in 1956 to construct SAGE, NORADS's Cold War computer network that coordinated data from multiple radar locations, one of the largest scale projects at the time.

Its name comes from the process flowing in one direction, downward like a waterfall, and has a fixed set of phases: conception, initiation, analysis, design, construction, testing, deployment, and maintenance.

The similarity with the assembly line process is self-evident, but back then, it was easy and natural for people to believe that this was the best way to build software. After all, it was a derivation of the most successful process of building things.

An Evolution

Manufacturing processes evolved, and the most significant change since the Taylor-Ford assembly line, funnily enough, also came from the automotive industry.

The Toyota Production System (TPS) was developed and perfected by Taiichi Ohno and Eiji Toyoda but was only made public in the early 1990s and was inspired by Taylor and Ford's observations on production inefficiencies.

As a testament to its merit, it is arguably recognized as the single factor that turned Toyota into the automotive industry leader for most of the last half-century.

TPS's effectiveness is attributed to its focus on eliminating or minimizing "the 3Ms"; *Muri*, *Mura*, and *Muda*, the Japanese words for overburden, inconsistency, and waste, respectively. Its goal is to have a dynamic process that can deliver results with the least effort, in a way that feels natural, by constantly tweaking it as you learn about its existing or newly acquired inefficiencies.

Toyota highlighted its underlying principles, known as "The Toyota Way," as follows:

- Continuous improvement.
- Respect for people.
- The right process will produce the right results.
- Add value to the organization by developing your people and partners.
- Continuously solving root problems drives organizational learning.

Going into details on differences between Ford's assembly line and "The Toyota Way" is beyond the scope of this book, but there are two main differences that are not self-evident and worth highlighting:

1. Everyone involved and impacted by the process has a say in it and are invited to help improve it.

2. The process is intentionally designed to be dynamic. There's no recipe. Each product demands its own variation and should adapt as frequently and fast as inefficiencies are found.

This was a clear break from the do-as-you're-told policy of Ford's time, as people were now given autonomy to influence the results they were accountable for.

The "Toyota Production System," while not perfect and subject to a fair amount of criticism, was a big improvement on the methods of the time. It was so impactful that it led to a second manufacturing revolution and became the new standard.

Its more generalized form, known as "Lean Manufacturing," trickled down to many sectors and morphed into several industry-specific versions like "Lean Construction" and "Lean Higher Education," among others.

It also gave birth to a new SDLC called "Lean Software Development," popularized by the eponymous book "Lean Software Development: An Agile Toolkit[14]" by Mary and Tom Poppendieck. It was also one of the key inspirations for the creation of methodologies like Agile Software Development, often just called Agile, SCRUM, and more.

TLC's influence in Today's software development practices is pervasive. Concepts like Kaizen, roughly translated to continuous improvement, led to the creation of rituals like "retrospectives" and practices like Continuous Integration. Kanban, also the name of an SDLC methodology, led to the adoption of Backlogs.

The Root of the Problem

At this point, the reader might see a clash of opinions—on the one hand, we argue that the complexity of projects makes upfront planning a futile exercise. On the other hand, we state the same set of processes, with over a hundred years of successful track record, works very well.

Where does the difference lie? It lies in what one tries to build: software vs. physical products.

We previously discussed companies' typical planning and prioritization approaches and the issues around them.

---

[14] "Lean Software Development: An Agile Toolkit", ISBN 978-0321150783

It's fair to highlight that the issues mentioned often stem from companies using processes and practices conceived for manufacturing goods (turning raw materials into finished physical products)—particularly outdated ones.

At first glance, this might seem non-consequential, but there are some fundamental breaks between the two.

Product Development

In a manufacturing process, the word "development" does not have the same meaning as it does for software. Development means creating the initial designs, modeling each component, and verifying that all the parts work together to prove that the results are within the customer's specified requirements. In software engineering, we call this prototyping.

Because physical goods depend on physical resources, the consequent prohibitive costs of producing the wrong product at a scale that comes from it lead to much more time and investment spent in this stage on physical things than on software.

Verification and Validation (V&V)

V&V are two concepts that translate almost seamlessly from manufacturing to software engineering, and this is their simplest definition.

- Verification: The process of checking that a product works as it's expected to, without technical issues (bugs)
- Validation: The process of checking whether the product attends the user needs it's supposed to (requirements)

Or, as Barry Boehm, software engineer and one of the first researchers of software development and quality control processes, wisely put:

- Verification asks, **are we building the product right?**
- Validation asks, **are we building the right product?**

The key property of digital products that is harder to test for V&V than physical ones is called falsifiability, or the complexity of proving that something is wrong.

A plane has to fly, a ball has to roll, and a door needs to open and close. While those are simplifications, the nature of the tests one can apply to something physical is somewhat limited. Even subjective properties of products like taste, aroma, and texture can be subjected to tests that are still deterministic. These characteristics make defining if a physical item is built "correctly" or it is "working" straightforward. With software, things are far from being this simple.

Beyond non-functional requirements, like safety, security, performance, etc., the definition of "correct" is open to interpretation.

Who's to say that a feature truly addresses a user's need or is the best way to solve a problem? Or even harder, that it's the best implementation given the context?

Software is malleable, after all—that's the "soft" part of the name and is the root of why process design to build "things" don't work as well for building "information."

- It also doesn't require a physical resource, so it's harder to pinpoint waste.

- It's comparatively more uncomplicated to put in front of users than physical products, which makes the work put into prototyping and validation a relatively higher cost of its total lifecycle.

- Software malleability also enables higher competition, which in turn increases the pressure for time-to-market, which in turn can force people to cut corners.

All these factors, as unintuitive as they are, are the reason and the root of so much frustration felt by developers all around the world as the concept of project management is so poorly understood and its complexity understated.

An efficient engineering manager, one that gets things done, needs to appreciate these complexities because they have a direct impact on the life of the people they lead and can make a difference between their careers being successful or not.

A Lean Project Management

So, here's the Billion dollar question: How to reconcile the fluidic nature of software, its inherent complexity, and the challenges of development processes while making a project more likely to be successful?

A clue can be found in the TPM originally called *just-in-time production*, or JIT, as in "making only what is needed, only when it is needed, and only in the amount that is needed."

As the story goes, Taiichi Ohno, who's considered the father of JIT, got the inspiration from visiting an American supermarket. Then he observed how the shelves were replenished at the same pace customers were picking items from them.

In his view, this ensured that there was no excess or shortage of products which, consequently, led to maximizing sales, conserving resources, and setting the pace for resupplying the store. In summa, the elimination of waste.

The high complexity of software development, exhaustively explored previously, can be tackled with the diligent application of JIT.

While Lean Software Development is one of the closest SDLC methodologies to JIT, and we encourage the reader to learn more about it, the core concept is what matters—just do what you need right now.

Let's now look at a JIT-like project management approach for developing software.

The Lean Inception

An *Inception* is an activity done at the beginning and whenever possible, at every step of a project to get everyone impacted together and

- Create alignment around goals.
- Define what needs to be done in the current iteration.
- Set the ground rules of collaboration.
- Discuss the current state of things and adjust expectations.
- Make changes in the scope or processes to maximize the chances of success.

The Lean Inception (LI) is a set of practices developed for inception targeting software development. It was created by Paulo Caroli and described in his excellent book: *Lean Inception: How to Align People and Build the Right Product.*[15]

LI was created as a tool to quickly define a project's Minimum Viable Product, commonly referred to as an MVP.

Eric Ries, author, and creator of the "Lean Startup" movement, defines MVPs as *"that version of a new product which allows a team to collect the maximum amount of validated learning about customers with the least effort."*

Applying JIT to software development with successful project management is achieved by *building your product as a series of MVPs and adjusting the product and process as you learn until you reach the project's goals.*

This approach has many benefits, with the most obvious being *making it easier to tackle complexity.*

---

[15] "Lean Inception: How to Align People and Build the Right Product", ISBN 978-8594377135

As Desmond Tutu, Nobel Peace Prize laureate for his work on anti-apartheid, once wisely said: *"there is only one way to eat an elephant: a bite at a time."*

Complex problems can be dealt with if we break them down into smaller, more manageable parts.

But beyond that, this incremental approach to software development has three other benefits that are particularly important for remote development teams:

1. Increased engagement
2. Minimization of issues coming out of misunderstanding
3. Maximization of the delivery of value to the business

Engagement is one of the least discussed aspects of this process but the most crucial in our experience. The second and third benefits might not be achievable without engagement or at least become severely compromised.

That said, the best way to achieve engagement is by continually releasing value to the business, which we often do through the release of features.

Most people organically commit to doing their best work, supervised or not, when they see a frequent flow of changes gradually but steadily, making the product better, the users happier, the business achieving its goals, and getting constant recognition.

This "happy state" makes all the complexities of building software projects, amplified in remote environments, much more manageable.

We now offer the readers suggestions of how to apply these concepts in real life. You can use this as a starting point, but keep in mind that this is a condensed version, therefore not complete and ignoring many caveats.

In Practice

Before Starting Projects

Before a project starts, there are three activities that, when done correctly, help to steer the course of the project toward success.

First – Select the Core Team

We suggest electing at least three people, one for each of the following roles:

1. A Sponsor: The person who requested or approved the project, usually someone involved in strategy

2. A Lead: The one responsible for the project's execution, usually the Engineering Manager

3. A Validator: The one responsible for making decisions around the project from a business perspective, often the Product Manager

While the same person can do those roles, we advise against it. Conflict of interest arising from a person wearing multiple hats is well-documented.

Second – Define Stakeholders

Beyond the core team, we need to map and understand clearly who the stakeholders are because there's very little chance of this, or any process, working well without that.

Map the people holding crucial information, subject matter experts, and those impacted by the execution of the project directly or not.

Third – Set Your Success Criteria

Identify the success metrics for the project and make them visible. This doesn't have to be measurable (although it helps a lot), but it needs to be something that can work as a compass to help tell if the project is going in the right direction.

It can be as objective as a Key Performance Indicator, or KPI, or as subjective as user happiness.

The Liftoff Meetings

Involving Everyone Impacted

This is pretty self-explanatory, but there are caveats worth mentioning:

- The more people you have in the room, the more chances for opinions to clash. Assigning the roles we mentioned helps to address that, as they can work as the voice for others.

- There's no need for consensus, just agreement on the general objectives. In case of hard disputes, use the Sponsor or Lead to work as mediators and tie breakers.

- Define clearly the difference between who's involved and who's committed. This helps during discussions and decision-making.

- Rule of thumb: People committed are those responsible for the execution and success of the project and are accountable if it fails. Everyone else is just involved.

- Set regular checkpoint meetings, or mini-inceptions, if you will. Use those for temperature checks and, if necessary, course correction. Do that as soon as possible so people can work it into their schedules.

Lean inception was originally conceived to be a weeklong workshop, and while this is reasonable for large projects, it'll be overkill for the ones of small or medium size.

Instead, try to compile LIs core sessions into two or three partial day sessions to keep with its spirit but maximize everyone's time.

We suggest the following flow:

Meeting 0 – With the Team

- Have a high-level overview of the project's goals, motivations, and impacts on the business and team.

- Start motivating everyone.

- Set initial expectations.
    - For the team as a group
    - For each individual in private

Meeting 1 – With the Team and Stakeholders

- Explain the process to everyone involved without too many details.

- Set the ground rules for collaboration, and have it documented.

- Invite the client or someone speaking on their behalf, often the validator, to explain the problem the project is trying to solve.

- Ask for people tangentially involved to add to the discussion.

- Have each team member take individual notes.

Meeting 2 – With the Team

- Milestone and Epics breakdown. Try splitting the project into small deliverables with high business values.

- Sticky notes session with everyone raising possible solutions and then grouping the different ideas into themes.

  - Common post-its usually indicate stories, but those should not be discussed during this meeting.

- Common themes eventually become Epics.

- Connect themes can be grouped into Milestones.

- Finish the meeting with a team agreement around Milestones; no need to agree on the Epics (or even spend much time on them).

Suggestions:

- Prioritize first the things (Epics, Milestones) with high certainty.

- For the one with less certainty, shelve the discussions around them, unless they are foundational to the project, then schedule timeboxed research stories.

- Prioritize then things with high value for the business and low complexity unless they're foundational.

- Treat each Milestone as an MVP in the sense it delivers the max business value with the least effort.

  - If necessary, break the milestones into multiple versions to allow for a fast-paced release cycle.

Meeting 3 – Team and Stakeholders

- Present the result of the previous meeting in a condensed way.

- Focus on Milestones and some focal Story/Epics to give some sense of depth.

- Get an agreement and sign-off from those you need.

- Assuming all's well, you're ready to start the project.
- If not, rinse and repeat Meeting 2–3 (or 1) until you're ready.

Suggestions:

- Keep the milestones as simple as possible and with clear goals.
- Even if the project has many clear milestones, choose just a few (2–4) to be your project's Version 1. This way, you create a clear checkpoint to review, regroup and reprioritize things based on the learnings captured along the project.

Starting the Project

Start reviewing the material from the previous meetings and having a free-form conversation about what's required to achieve the Milestone goals with minimum effort. It goes without saying, but I'll say it anyway, compromise on scope, not quality.

Go over the sticky notes of the initial story and milestone breakdown, and use it as a starting point but focus on the first milestone only.

The way we're working, we create stories for milestones only when we're about to start working on them. This ensures fresh context for everyone involved, and you can leverage the learnings of a previous milestone to have a more constructive conversation. That said, not every team might be apt or enjoy working this way. Play to your strengths (and weaknesses) to decide the format, but I suggest giving it a try.

Writing Stories

When creating stories, try to follow a linear and incremental flow with stories complementing each other. Start with any foundational stories and go from there.

Try to make the stories as small as possible as long as they deliver some value. Arbitrarily breaking down stories to make them small is a common anti-pattern that should be avoided whenever possible. Some caveats and things worth noting:

- This model can lead to bottlenecks, especially in the beginning.
- Some suggestions to deal with that are:

- Pairing. Helps with knowledge sharing, which is a great side-benefit

- Leaving a buffer of stories that people could pick from to account for that

- Tech debts or off-sprint activities

- This can lead to good parallelization if played well.

Try writing as little as possible for the stories themselves and avoid technical details. The story should contain:

- What's the problem we're trying to solve

- Who's going to benefit from it

- Why are we doing it

- List of criteria for a story to be accepted

Other information can be provided but trying to write the solution on the same story tends to lock it down while leaving it open allows for some level of freedom for those implementing it.

When discussing the stories, allow each person to write what they think the story should be after the team discusses its overall goals. This allows them to think from a different perspective, think about the business implications, and be more critical of what's required for it to be completed (especially when writing down acceptance criteria), and it's more engaging to everyone.

One last thing worth noticing is to try separating stories from tasks. Tasks are specific things that need to get done, stories are small, self-sufficient steps we need to take to achieve something bigger.

Running the Sprint

The stories should be prioritized before the sprint starts. The planning meeting should take care of it, and grooming sessions, a moment to review stories and check on the state of things, allow for changes that might have happened meanwhile.

Try setting sprint goals whenever possible and ask the team what they are willing to commit to. This creates a psychological deadline that will help people to be more critical of unplanned work, scope changes, or external noise. It should at least be helpful to make those things more visible, especially when coupled with a "Sprint Goal check" during stand-up.

As the team members pick stories to work on and they get done, deliver in a badge fashion to your validator or lead so they can try it out and give feedback. Unbadge after they approve or the time of roll out for the feature is right.

Some teams create private slack rooms to ask for this kind of feedback. This has the side effect of increasing engagement around everyone involved in the project, which can lead to great shoutouts.

In case you use external validators, like clients or members of other teams, let developers ask for feedback themselves and try to deal with the users directly, as that creates great morale, and act on the background to make adjustments. Keep track of the users' feedback, separating them into

- Immediate feedback – things that need to be changed in a current story or meaningful things on stories recently released.

- Must-haves – things that impact the Milestone currently being worked on or upcoming Milestone.

- Nice-to-haves – good ideas in need of more research that could feedback into the business pipeline. We call that our Icebox.

Review all those feedback with our stakeholders during your checkpoint meetings to get more information and adjust expectations (except the immediate ones that might have been tackled already by the time we meet with them).

Closing Milestones

During checkpoint meetings, get official signoff from stakeholders until you acknowledge that the milestone is completed, by reviewing the goals and checking if they were achieved.

Closing the Project

After each milestone, check if the project goals have been achieved. If it hasn't, pick the next milestone that takes you closer to the goal.

If it has, your project is done.

Things Left Unsaid

We believe that the topics discussed in this chapter can give you a good understanding of the challenges of an Engineering Manager. Still, while we think we provide a comprehensive view of what the role requires, there are two big topics that we're purposefully not covering: Career Development and Diversity, Equity, and Inclusion.

Career Management encompasses everything from professional development, to behavioral education, to promotions. It can vary wildly from company to company (just as the expectations around EM can be), and it's yet another important area without clear standards. We advise the reader to delve into the topic, discuss different approaches with seasoned managers, get a better understanding of how the process works in their organization, and start forming their critical thinking and framework to do career development when it comes effectively.

Last but definitely not least, comes Development and Diversity, Equity, and Inclusion, or DEI.

An (inevitably) crude overview of the topic:

Diversity is the presence of differences like race, gender, sexual orientation, nationality, and much more. A significant source of conflict, frustration, and, sometimes, commercial failure arises from not seeing and understanding these differences, therefore not accepting and including said differences in the conversation.

Equity is enabling fairness and giving different people similar chances. A fair misunderstanding around equity is thinking everyone should be treated the same, but in reality, it means people should have the same opportunities. An anecdote to illustrate this can be thought of as having a marathon and giving everyone the same shoes as giving everyone a shoe that fits.

Inclusion is making sure people feel welcomed in a community, not despite their differences but because of them, and are able to participate in the decision-making process equitably.

A great read on DEI is the book "Just Work: Get Sh*t Done, Fast and Fair" by Tim Scott. It focuses on six dimensions of bias that might be present in a work setting (three at an individual level, three at a systems level) while discussing her personal experiences with biases and that of her peers.

Career Development and DEI are likely some of the most exciting and challenging parts of the life of an EM, and we can't stress enough that you'd be in a league of your own if you get good at them.

Conclusion

Managing people and projects are difficult tasks.

As a developer, showing a certain level of frustration or dissatisfaction might be tolerated, permitted, or, at times, even encouraged. Once you are responsible for facilitating interactions between people, you will set the tone.

Consequently, your work life will become more political, and your impact will take a while to show, albeit it'll likely be more meaningful and long-lasting.

You will be switching from a "hands-on job" (direct impact) to a "hands-off" job (working through others). That does not mean that you will be doing less work; on the contrary. But it does mean that the nature of your work changes considerably. A large part of your job becomes behavioral rather than practical. Being present, listening to people, protecting your team, and creating and shaping an atmosphere conducive to collaboration require you to adopt new habits and develop new skills.

These might come naturally to some people, but most of us need to train these skills. For example, not becoming involved in minute details (i.e., not micromanaging) can become difficult since "minute details" have been your bread and butter as an individual contributor throughout your entire past.

There is no silver bullet to becoming a good manager. Like in any profession, it takes time and experience, and the best way to gain this experience is to first work under others who know their trade well.

This way, you can gradually take over responsibility, safely try things, and practice your new skills with support and experience to guide you so that when the time is right, you're well prepared to formally leap into management.

So, Should You Become a Manager?

After reading all this, you might be discouraged from taking on this role. The complexity, the challenges, and the discomfort might look like too much.

But maybe you're exactly the right person for the job.

In software engineering, bad managers often are those lacking practical experience in the field, never working under others doing the job they're now managing. They never saw the other side of the fence.

Managers without technical experience never have to hone the skills that would later allow them to maintain technical oversight, manage expectations and deal with the complexity of hard problems.

It also meant that they never truly understood what it takes to build solid systems or what the effort entails, which, in turn, can make them difficult people to work for and with.

Explaining basic concepts to the people you report to, can be frustrating, making it harder to relate, discuss solutions, and reason with them. It also makes it extra hard for you to justify decisions and can lead to frustrating disagreements as they are inefficient at mediating technical discussions.

On the other hand, having worked as a developer, you can recognize technical teams' challenges, empathize uniquely, and be more successful than most in guiding groups to success.

Also, non-technical managers of technical teams never lived through the result of making bad technical decisions as engineers. They were never bitten by the problems that they created. Consequently, they struggle to identify wrong choices and flawed technical justifications and are not as willing to innovate as they incur risks they don't fully grasp.

All of this has a very personal consequence. It means that a team is no longer ruled by meritocracy as the most competent people are no longer free to advance the product in the best way possible. It's now a team governed by politics. The friendliest, most eloquent, or political engineer would win an argument where introverts would likely lose their voices.

Every field needs capable people in leadership positions. In the software engineering world, this could be you. Throughout the rest of this book, we'll help you to understand how to go from an outstanding engineer to an exceptional engineering manager.

Hiring

[An expert] is someone who knows some of the worst mistakes that can be made in his subject and knows how to avoid them

—Werner Heisenberg

Behind every great business, there are great people. No matter how automated a business is or to whom you are providing the goods and services, without good people, your business will fail. Competence and incompetence permeate every layer of your organization. From top to bottom. A good teammate can lift everybody up, while a few bad apples have the power to kill every last morsel of passion, enthusiasm, and collaboration. Bad apples will destroy products faster than good people can build them. As such, hiring the right people is self-evident, no matter what industry you are in. But that is easier said than done. As any recruiter can attest to, finding good professionals is difficult, and often the difficulties begin by actually trying to define what a right fit looks like for your business. Hence we begin this chapter with the latter: What do we mean with the *"right people"*?

Defining "Right People"

By "right" we mean a person that satisfies the following criteria:

1. **Has the required technical knowledge to perform the expected activities**

    This should be obvious, yet we all know this one colleague whom we could not trust to make even a cup

B. Jakobus et al., *Leadership Paradigms for Remote Agile Development*, https://doi.org/10.1007/978-1-4842-8719-4_4

of coffee. A common pitfall that results in the hiring of this colleague is the focus on key words in the resume, instead of careful scrutiny. The most effective way to ensure a high level of technical talent is to create high barriers of entry. That is, make technical exercises and technical interviews challenging, and design them in such a way as to best reflect the requirements of the role. Except for the most junior roles, take-home technical exercises that only take an hour or two are often too short to correctly classify candidates. Similarly, a single, 1-hour long, technical interview will most likely not allow you to collect sufficient signals to determine whether or not the candidate is a good fit. Remember that the purpose of the interview process is not to find the perfect candidate or to push as many candidates through the pipeline as possible. Instead, the purpose of the interview process is to filter out unsuitable candidates.

When it comes to solemnly technical abilities, we found the most effective technical interview process to contain:

2. **A complex take-home exercise** which accurately reflects the working environment and project requirements, and which candidates can do in their own time. Make the exercise technically challenging, but ensure that these challenges are similar to those that the candidate would face on a daily basis. Avoid brain-teasers and math problems unless that is the type of problems that they will be solving daily. Ask candidates to include tests and focus on good code quality. Once completed, ask them to submit the exercise using a version control system. Mirror submission to day-to-day interaction.

3. **A technical interview in which candidates need to talk through their submitted solution,** justifying their decisions, design, and architecture. Here it is important that you dive into the details, and try to expose as much of the candidate's background as possible. Sometimes decisions that seem small were carefully thought through and can show how thorough a candidate can be. Usually, this type of interview lasts 1-2 hours and gives enough room to allow the candidate to ask questions. Remember: the type of questions a candidate asks can tell you a lot about their level of experience.

4. **An additional systems-design interview round**[1] that lasts roughly 1 hour (applicable only when hiring more senior candidates). This allows you to evaluate the candidate's overall level of experience, beyond the narrow focus of the job. A good software engineer should have a solid, all-around understanding of how a system is built and structured. They should understand how to model data, what security considerations need to be taken into account when building a system, how to choose and reason about different technologies, as well as understand the impact of their decisions and potential gray areas. Good candidates will understand what trade-offs to make between the frontend and backend, and how this affects the overall product.

5. **Is capable of anticipating problems before they happen**

   Mistakes are costly—both in terms of time, money, and morale. A good software engineer not only solves problems, but is able to anticipate them before they occur. They are proactive rather than reactive. While there are plenty of experienced professionals that are not capable of anticipating problems, years of experience can usually be one solid indicator: Younger engineers have often not lived through enough of their own mistakes to spot problems before they occur. Older engineers, in contrast, have almost certainly been bitten by their own decisions.

   Being able to anticipate problems not only means having lived through one's mistakes. It also means being able to reason within an environment that contains high levels of uncertainty. We will discuss this in detail later on in this chapter (see section "The Importance of Experience"), but in essence it comes down to this: People that do well in environments with high levels of uncertainty are people that are good at estimating probabilities (subconsciously or otherwise). Unfortunately, more than half a century of research in psychology shows that the majority of people are terrible at this. Calibration tests are one

---

[1] It is important to note that a systems design interview question does not always need to be posed as such. Asking "how would you implement, or scale, your [take home] in production?" may be equally valid, depending on the circumstance.

commonly used method of measuring how good somebody is at estimating probabilities. While some professionals such as weather forecasters[2] are quite good at estimating probabilities, most people are not.[3] One possible explanation for this is outlined eloquently by Lichtenstein et al. as they summarize Pitz' (1974) research:[4]

"Pitz (1974), too, accepted that people's information-pro-cessing capacity and working memory capacity are limited. He suggested that people tackle complex problems serially, working through a portion at a time. To reduce cognitive strain, people ignore the uncertainty in their solutions to the early portions of the problem in order to reduce the com-plexity of the calculations in later portions."

Calibration testing aside, finding candidates that are good at dealing with uncertainty is difficult. Diving deep into a candidate's background and designing well-prepared systems design interview questions weed out the most unsuitable candidates.

6. **Is humble and self-conscious**

    Nobody knows everything. Good professionals are aware of their limitations and act this way. That is, they perform their tasks carefully. They are able to learn from their shortcomings as well as accept advice and suggestions from other team members. Arrogance incurs a large cost on both the team and the product, as arrogant engineers are not only difficult to work with, but are often incapable of accepting thoughts and improvements coming from others. On the other hand, humble engineers are almost by definition good team players. In an interview, this is a difficult trait to test for. Therefore, instead of actively trying to find a humble candidate, filter out those that are clearly not humble. Huge red flags are candidates that

    - Have difficulties speaking about times when they were part of a team.

---

[2] Murphy AH, Winkler RL (1977) Reliability of subjective probability forecasts of precipita-tion and temperature. J R Stat Soc C Appl Stat 26(1):41–47
[3] "Risk Intelligence: How to Live with Uncertainty" by Dylan Evans, ISBN-10: 9781451610918
[4] "Judgment under uncertainty: heuristics and biases" (Cambridge 600 University Press, Cambridge, pp 306–33)

- Always refer to themselves and never speak of their team. Sentences begin with "I," never with "we".

- Speak badly of their past company or teammates.

- Are unable to discuss solutions or accept direction/suggestions as part of questions in the technical interview process.

- Are unable to identify their own limitations;

- Use specific technologies/frameworks as escape hatches to avoid showing that they do not know something (as opposed to discussing a topic holistically).

7. **Possesses good analytical skills**

Having good analytical skills does not only mean that the person is able to gather relevant information to solve the problem. It also means being able to properly scope a problem. That is, being able to identify what is not part of the problem. Engineers that are not able to draw accurate boundaries will inevitably implement solutions that are unnecessarily complex while also spending company time (i.e., money) implementing things that are not needed.

Furthermore, engineers with high analytical skills are able to test and experiment with data, and draw accurate conclusions based on this data. Being able to understand a problem is not very useful in itself if you are not able to evaluate your solution.

When it comes to identifying candidates with strong analytical skills, the systems design interview question is critical. Not only does the question help gauge a candidate's overall level of experience and technical abilities, but it also provides insight into how a candidate bisects and reasons about problems. Candidates that do well on system design interview questions demonstrate that they can accurately identify requirements and establish boundaries.

Alongside the systems design interview question, presenting candidates with a dataset which they need to analyze helps filter out candidates that possess lower levels of analytical skills.

8. **Are good communicators**

Any book, article, or podcast on management, leadership, or interviews will tell you about the importance of good communication skills. As such, we do not want to spend much time on an already exhausted topic. Good communication skills are critical. Period. Professionals that are good communicators

- Give straight answers (No BS)

- Are polite and honest

- Are able to handle conflict when divergent opinions arise

- Are able to give and receive feedback

- Are able to discuss and justify their decisions and solutions

- Are humble and self-conscious (i.e., able to admit when they are wrong and aware of their own limitations)

- Are reachable. That is, they respond to and act on messages in a timely manner as appropriate

The "Good Engineer" Checklist

As shown in Figure 4-1, aside from the aforementioned core pillars that define a good professional, good software engineers are

- Action biased instead of overplanners.

- Iterators. They understand the importance of iterative development and realize that as long as a contribution improves the system, that contribution does not need to be perfect. Continuous iteration results in constant improvements.

- Capable of breaking down larger concepts/problems into smaller ones.

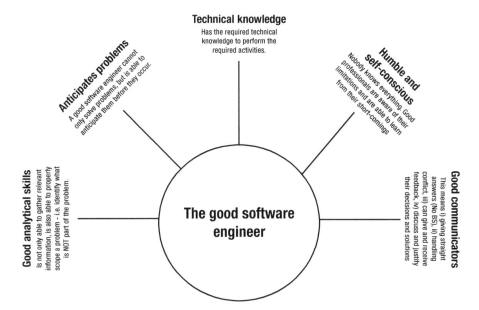

Figure 4-1. The good software engineer in a nutshell

The "Bad Engineer" Checklist

A bad engineer is basically the inverse of the previous two sections. Here is a list of behaviors commonly found in underperforming professionals. These behaviors are the direct consequence of a lack of the attributes described in the previous section and are summarized in Figure 4-1.

The bad engineer:

- Cannot justify decisions technically.

- Is not disciplined.

- Is unreliable. For example, they agree to something in a meeting, but then go away and forget to action on the agreed or do something completely different altogether without communicating this change.

- Does not incorporate advice, comments, or industry best practices.

- Ignores feedback. This not only makes interactions with the professional frustrating for others, but actually means that they are unwilling to learn. They lack the technical background for the job, but are so uncooperative that they are unable to gain these skills.

- Offloads work on to other people's shoulders and has to be "carried" by the team.

- Does not interact during meetings or fails to attend meetings in the first place.

- Is unable to give an insight into the progress of their work/estimate when things will be done. When asked, they either give an overly general answer, or go into pointless minute details.

- Is not proactive, only reactive.

- Masks incompetence by using arrogance or other subterfuge like job titles, department responsibilities, etc.

- Lacks attention to detail and acts in a generally negligent manner. Attention to detail when performing one task generally means lack of attention in general. As an old saying goes: "How we do one thing is how we do everything else." That is, people that tend to greatly underperform in one area of their job tend to do so in all other areas of their job too.

- Lacks pride and interest in their work.

- Is not able to think through problems.

Keep in mind that the points listed above are behaviors that bad engineers do consistently, great engineers can have a bad day and slip into those behaviors occasionally but they certainly shouldn't be a habit for them.

 Info   Attitude trumps lack of technical background in most jobs. That is, with the right attitude, we can learn to excel at a job. However, a characteristic of an underperforming engineer is that they lack both the right attitude AND technical background/knowledge. Without the right attitude, they are unable to learn the skills they lack.

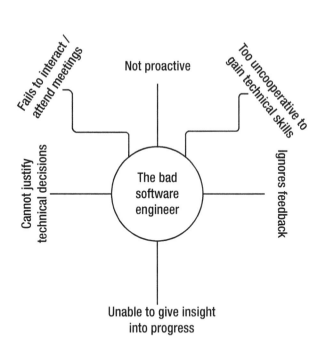

Figure 4-2. The bad software engineer in a nutshell

The Importance of Experience

The Cambridge English dictionary defines experience[5] as the process of doing and seeing things and of having things happen to you. In other words, people with experience are those whose thoughts and actions have been shaped by both their own past and the past of others. Life experience allows us to

- Live through other people's decisions

- Make decisions without all the necessary data

- Know the importance of decisions and how they might affect the future

In slightly more complex terms: experience allows us to deal with uncertainty. Most importantly, "unknown unknowns." That is, it enables us to deal with the correlation between experience and a broader knowledge that decreases the surface of things that we do not even know we don't know (unknown unknowns). In his book "Risk Intelligence," Dr. Dylan Evans illustrates this notion (depicted in Figure 4-3) using the concept of a darkened room:

---

[5] https://dictionary.cambridge.org/us/dictionary/english/experience

"Picture your mind as a lightbulb shining in an otherwise dark room. Some nearby objects are fully illuminated; you can see them in every detail, present and identifiable. They are the things you know very well: the names of your friends, what you had for breakfast this morning, how many sides a triangle has, and so on. The objects on the other side of the room are completely shrouded in darkness. They are the things about which you know nothing: the five thousandth digit of pi, the composition of dark matter, King Nebuchadnezzar's favorite color. Between light and darkness, however, lies a gray area in which the level of illumination gradually shades away. In this twilight zone, the objects are not fully illuminated, but neither are they completely invisible."

Assuming that an individual learns from both their past experiences and the experiences of others, they will, with time, become better at navigating this twilight zone. That is what we mean when we say that "experience allows professionals to deal with uncertainty." Note that this does not imply that the twilight zone will shrink with experience. Of course it might if the individual remains in the same domain for years and gathers more and more minute knowledge. But in most cases, the twilight zone will always remain—people switch jobs, tackle new challenges, or venture into new domains. With experience however, the individuals become more self-aware of their limitations, the limitations of their field as well as how much relevant information they may not have to make a decision. Over and under-confidence are replaced with better self-knowledge, and the individual becomes "better calibrated" to their task environment. Not only does this allow for more effective task execution as risks and uncertainties can be identified more readily, it also makes for better communication: The more experienced someone is in a field, the better their educated guesses and probability estimates become.

In contrast, inexperienced professionals might have learned the necessary technical skills to execute a task that lies "outside the twilight zone," but they usually are unable to make (or even identify) far-reaching decisions and voice them with the right amount of certainty. Without having been bitten by their own mistakes a sufficient number of times, inexperience means bringing either a *"dangerous excess or a problematic deficiency"*[6] to the table. An inexperienced candidate has not had the time to make all the mistakes that they need to make. Since they do not know what these mistakes are (or how to avoid them), chances are that they will make at least some while working on your project.

---

[6] "Risk Intelligence", Dr. Dylan Evans, page 24

It is therefore no surprise that experience is highly valued in the field of software engineering. Engineers can make multiple important decisions in a short time frame that will deeply impact the future of an entire project, especially in the initial phases of a project. Therefore having a good understanding of the consequences of those decisions in the future, the knowns, unknowns, and unknown unknowns, will directly impact the success of the project.

To put this all into more concrete terms: There are decisions that are easy to change later, like choosing a certain existing library for a very specific feature. However, other types of decisions, such as selecting a programming language or framework for a project, are much harder to change or revert. Experience plays an important role in this context, as it not only allows the engineer to properly differentiate between the different types of decisions, but also enables the engineer to handle difficult decisions more effectively. That is, when making a decision that is difficult to revert in the future, they can take the necessary steps that could make a potential reversal less difficult. For example, applying different techniques to properly isolate code and hence minimizing the impact of future changes.

Decision making and uncertainty aside, experience also acts as a natural filter for unsuitable job candidates. As Tim Nichols concisely puts it in *"The Death of Expertise"*:[7]

"Every field has its trials by fire, and not everyone survives them, which is why experience and longevity in a particular area or profession are reasonable markers of expertise."

---

[7] page 33

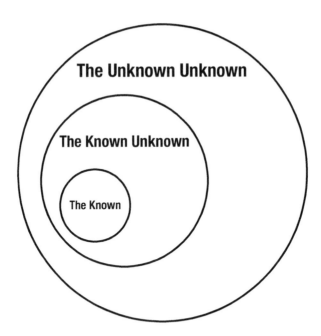

Figure 4-3. An illustration of Dr. Evan's "Darkened Room."

The Dunning-Kruger Effect

We probably all know this one incompetent colleague who was consistently unable to deliver, but thought the world of themselves. It turns out that there is a name for this type of illusory superiority: the Dunning-Kruger effect. First proposed in the late 1990s by two psychologists, David Dunning and Justin Kruger,[8] the effect basically states that the incompetent are unaware of their incompetences due to the lack of competence (Figure 4-4). Put more bluntly: the stupid are too stupid to realize that they are stupid. For example, an incompetent software engineer may be

---

[8] Kruger J, Dunning D. Unskilled and unaware of it: how difficulties in recognizing one's own incompetence lead to inflated self-assessments. J Pers Soc Psychol. 1999 Dec;77(6):1121-34. doi: 10.1037//0022-3514.77.6.1121. PMID: 10626367.

unaware of their inability to design and write good software, since the very skills that would allow them to develop such software are the same skills that allow them to identify "bad" software. The irony therefore follows that, in order to make a bad software engineer realize their incompetence, they must become more competent.

While, according to Dunning and Kruger, the incompetent are overconfident in their abilities, the more competent a person becomes, the more underconfident they become, as through knowledge they become blissfully aware of the limits of their knowledge. It is therefore no surprise that many companies profess "humility" as one of the core values that they look for in candidates. Sure, the "overconfident know it all" will be an annoying colleague and make for a bad culturefit. But at the heart of the boasting and bold candidates often lies a lack of knowledge and competence. Attributes such as "humility" and "modesty," on the other hand, are often a signal for competence and should be actively screened for when hiring.

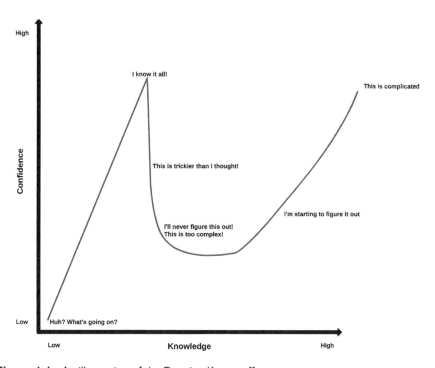

Figure 4-4. An illustration of the Dunning-Kruger effect

Honesty

Finding new hires is expensive (as we will see in the next section "The Cost of Hiring"). To ensure that these expenditures pay off (that is, to ensure that you actually retain your new hires), honesty during the interview process is crucial. Expecting job applicants to talk honestly and openly about their past experiences is a given. Unfortunately, many employers do not see honesty as a two-way street. Sugar-coating the position and company is common practice, either because the interviewer does not want to sound too negative (and hence be responsible for painting the company in a bad light) or because they are afraid of failing to attract the right candidate. This is problematic in two ways. Firstly, by lying, you are acting unethically. As Sam Harris eloquently puts it in his book "Lying," when he writes that *"[by lying] we deny others a view of the world as it is. Our dishonesty not only influences the choices they make, it often determines the choices they can make—and in ways we cannot always predict. Every lie is a direct assault upon the autonomy of those we lie to."*

That is, by sugar-coating a position, you deny the candidate to see what they are actually signing up for. Since people spend most of our waking hours at work, a candidate's understanding of the company will have a significant impact on their life if this understanding turns out to be false.

Secondly, by lying to candidates, you will end up generating additional costs for the company, as honesty and expectations are closely linked. You are hiring intelligent, capable candidates. And—surprise surprise—smart candidates will soon figure out what is wrong with the company. You, in turn, will gain a reputation as a dishonest leader, and will lose the trust of those working for you. A lack of trust combined in a company that fails to meet expectations results in brain drain: If the job market permits, people will leave. Which means you will need to start the hiring cycle all over again.

One prevailing source of dishonesty in leaders comes from unfeasible targets. An honest leader, operating in an honest environment, will never purposely aim at unfeasible targets. Leaders that catch themselves thinking about a $50-100 billion valuation in 5 years while the company only has 500 users should ask themselves how honest they are with themselves. While your job as a leader requires you to remain positive even when in adverse circumstances, you should remember that there is a balance to be struck between positivity and realism. Especially in business, honesty and realism go hand in hand. As Ayn Rand once famously said: *"You can ignore reality, but you can't ignore the consequences of ignoring reality."*

Another common source of dishonesty stems from sugar-coating challenges. Leaders can be upfront about the technical and organizational challenges that await candidates without needing to put everything into a completely negative light. Unfortunately, most leaders prefer to try and make reality look better than it really is.

Summarizing these two major sources of dishonesty in interviews: If you can **be honest about the status quo and what the company is aiming at**, then you will be able to avoid a significant percentage of churn.

Furthermore, Being honest about the growth possibilities for the candidate within the company is equally as important as being honest about the status quo. Many companies love to brag about growth opportunities but in reality prefer outside hires over internal promotions. Therefore, if you are offering growth opportunity, be ready to answer (or even better: include it in the job description)

- Exactly what promotion opportunities does the company offer?

- What percentage of the current employees walked that path?

- How long would the candidate need to wait to be considered for a promotion?

- Does the company have a clear path for promotions for that position?

- Are the opportunities and the candidate's expectation in synchronism?

Info   The seven golden rules for successful technical interviews

---

1. Interviews are all about looking for signals. Try and gather as many signals as possible by

   a. Not dwelling on minute technical details

   b. Not dwelling on a candidate's mistakes. Move on quickly

   c. Ask for specifics. Dig deep

2. Structure your technical interviews so that you can quickly identify signals which indicate a candidate's

   a. Ability to break down and analyze problems

   b. Ability to abstract

   c. Concern for code organization, clarity, and maintainability

   d. Concern for testing

     e. General technical knowledge (not minute details)

     f. Concern for documentation and how to keep and transfer knowledge

3. Behavioral and cultural interviews should look for signals that indicate

     a. An openness to learning and constant improvement

     b. An ability to give and deal with feedback

     c. A willingness to compromise

     d. A general fit for the company's culture

4. Successful interviews require preparation on behalf of the interviewer. This means

     a. Creating a bank of possible questions to ask across interviews

     b. Creating a scorecard and template for notes

     c. Reading up on the candidate's background before the interview

     d. Recording feedback and notes either during the interview or as soon as possible after the interview

5. Be transparent. There is no point in over-selling the role just to have someone leave shortly after accepting an offer as the role does not meet expectations.

6. Be empathetic and positive. Regardless of the candidate's performance, you should ensure that the interview is a positive experience for the candidate. Negative interview experiences reflect badly on both you and the company.

7. Dive into details when required. If a candidate only gives a generalized response, dig deeper.

The Cost of Hiring

Hiring involves direct and indirect costs. The direct costs, such as man-hours spent by recruiters or advertising, are obvious and as such we won't elaborate on those here. The indirect costs however are more subtle, yet usually greater. Recruiters naturally like to push as many candidates through the pipeline as possible. This approach leads to lost engineering man-hours. Technical interviews need extensive preparation, and technical exercises require reviewing. By narrowing the pipeline—that is, detailing the exact job requirements as best as possible, as well as setting high screening standards—a company can reduce these costs.

Once a candidate is hired, they will need to be on-boarded. Not only is this engineering time that is spent not developing the product (opportunity cost), but the on-boarding phase is likely to introduce risks to the product. New bugs tend to be introduced as new engineers begin working in a new, unfamiliar environment. While this decreases over time, and good engineers will more than make up for the cost of hiring (otherwise they would not be hired), it is important to keep this cost in mind as companies with a high churn will pay a high price.

The cost of hiring increases the higher your churn is. Once you begin losing a certain percentage of your teams, you not only lose knowledge but also impact team morale and team processes. Even if you have perfect hand-over processes and perfect documentation, lost knowledge is difficult to get back and usually takes many months (or years). A loss in morale on the other hand can result in a snow-ball effect: colleagues leave and either bring others with them to the new company or motivate them directly or indirectly to jump ship.

Last but not least, processes die with people. People enter a company and bring with them new processes and establish these for different reasons, experienced professionals implement them knowing their pros and cons, while inexperienced ones do so because they are comfortable with it and want to mitigate changes. Hopefully, the new processes might make actual sense and improve things. However, many times they are introduced because people want to set a mark, be seen to be doing things, or simply because they are used to working this way. Regardless of the "why," the introduction of new processes by new hires can often fan an existing fire: People are creatures of habit and like working in ways that they are used to. A large influx of new hires and new processes can therefore increase dissatisfaction and result in further brain drain.

Summarizing the cost of hiring:

1. Hiring is complex and costly. There are both direct and indirect costs.

2. New hires can result in further churn.

3. Knowledge and morale lost will be difficult to regain.

Info The objective of the interview process is to weed out the unsuitable candidates. Interview processes is not made to find the perfect candidate. Only time can reveal this.

The Cost of Bad Engineers

Before we begin to discuss the price that a company pays for hiring "bad" engineers, we need to distinguish a bad engineer from a bad hire. On the surface, this difference might not be immediately obvious. Nevertheless, it is an important one to keep in mind, and the essence of it is this: Sometimes a hire might not be the ideal fit for a team/company, but could still be a good fit for another team/company. Every single one of us is subject to situational forces, meaning that our surroundings define and exert certain processes of transformation on our character, changing how we act and react to those around us. Put into one team, a certain engineer might excel at tasks that, if placed in a different team, they would perform poorly. Being able to differentiate the causes of poor performance—that is, poor performance due to their surroundings, or poor performance due to incompetence—is difficult and requires careful observation. The cost of bad engineers is therefore different to the costs associated with bad hires. The latter can often be rectified or compensated with relatively little change and poses a lower risk to the company as a whole. This is because bad fits are due to situational forces, while bad professionals are "bad" because they lack certain attitudes, abilities, skills, or intelligences that are required in order to excel at the job regardless of the team.

While bad fits are low risk, an accumulation of bad engineers can quickly break a product/project/company and is therefore the topic of this section. As the age-old saying goes: Regardless, each team member is a cog in the machine. And a single broken cog can cause the machine to break down. Specifically, a bad engineer will

- Have a detrimental impact on the code base and hence the product as a whole.

- Have a negative impact on team morale. A good engineer paired with a bad engineer in the same position will cause the good engineer to feel demotivated.

- Introduce architectural decisions that can be difficult to revert and which result in a domino effect: Problems in systems tend to cascade and accumulate (this is detailed in depth in "Chapter 5: Quality").

- Increase churn and burn-out rate. Bad employees increase the workload for others, since good engineers need to make up for the bad engineers. This leads to higher stress levels and load.

Above all, bad engineers that are allowed to persist in their positions will set bad precedents and lower the standard of the team as a whole. Most people tend to sink to their lowest acceptable levels of performance. By not removing unsuitable team members, leaders set a low bar and signal to others that poor performance is acceptable. Once settled, these behavioral and cultural habits can be difficult to reverse even if the responsible individuals have been removed.

Info   Bad habits are like mold. Spread by underperforming professionals, they affect company culture and are difficult to remove.

Therefore, if leaders want their software products to succeed, they need to take swift action if unsuitable hires make it through the interview process. Remember: while a single cog is important, it does not mean that it cannot be replaced. Faulty cogs need to be exchanged or the machine will break down.

> [There is] wisdom in the old Chinese warning to beware a craftsman who claims twenty years of experience when in reality he's only had one year of experience twenty times
>
> —"The Death of Expertise" by Tim Nichols (page 36)

Retention: Understanding the Career Cycle

By now we have hopefully convinced the reader that hiring is expensive. One important factor in reducing the cost of hiring is retention. That is, keeping good employees for as long as possible. Based on our experience, at the heart of retention, lies the understanding of the cyclical nature of careers (depicted in Figure 4-5), meaning that we live out our careers in cycles. Depending on the individual, the length of an individual cycle may vary—some people's careers consist of many cycles; other people's careers consist of few cycles; and some very rare individuals might only live through one cycle. Furthermore, the shape of the individual cycles themselves may differ greatly.

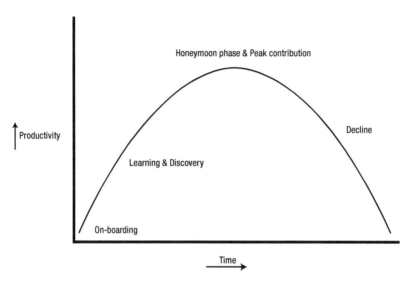

Figure 4-5. The career cycle

When we first join a company, our career enters the "on-boarding" phase: We do not yet know much about the technicals of the project we work on, the processes and internal workings of the company itself. As such, we are in a strong learning phase, and are not yet very productive. As time goes on, we become more familiar with our task environment and become more productive. We are enthusiastic, are constantly learning and discovering new things, and are trying to maximize our productivity and output. During the honeymoon phase, we see nothing "wrong" with our surroundings. We are dazzled by all the nice people around us and the world is our oyster—career opportunities glisten before us, and we put all our heart and energy into the job. We are at "peak contribution," meaning that we have learned a sufficient amount to be highly productive. As time goes on however, we start to see the cracks in the walls: politics, colleagues that we do not get on well with, a difficult boss, some big-picture decisions that we do not agree with, better pay elsewhere …Our enthusiasm wanes. Slowly we become used to the rut, and execute with less energy and enthusiasm. Stress might consume our remaining energy, and there isn't much to learn. We have entered the phase of decline. At the end of this phase, we either transition into a new role within the company (a promotion, a new team, or a new department) or we leave the company. Regardless of our decision, the cycle starts again.

The key to retention is therefore this: understand the cycle and realize when employees enter the phase of decline. Chances are you will never be able to prevent the decline phase (the world of work is too complex for this), but you will be able to stretch out the productivity and honeymoon phase a lot (see Figure 4.6 for examples of short and stretched out honeymoon phases).

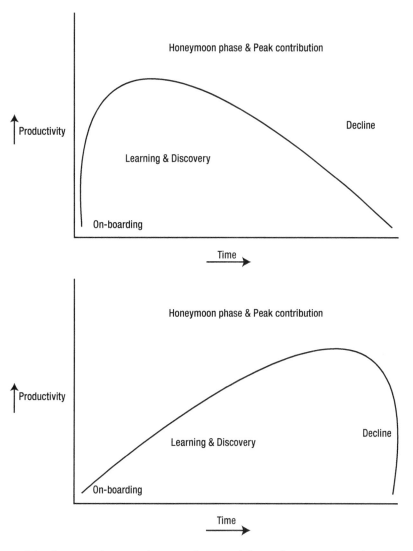

Figure 4-6. Career cycles can take many shapes and forms. Some people on-board quickly and contribute quickly, while others take some time to on-board and might quickly decline after

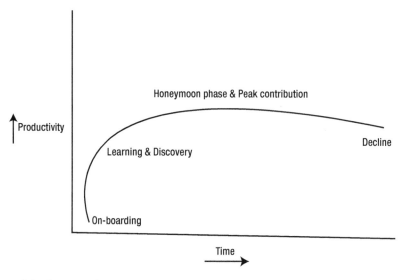

Figure 4-6. (continued)

The ideal cycle on-boards quickly and stretches out the honeymoon and peak phase for as long as possible, hence maximizing retention. Employees whose careers follow this shape remain productive in their positions for a long time, and only decline eventually.

Practical Tips

Hiring good engineers is easier said than done. And so far, we have done the easy part: We discussed hiring and retention in theoretical terms. Now comes the hard part: putting the theory into practice, and defining a set of concrete guidelines that you can apply immediately.

Tip 1: Review Your Interviewing Process

Many interviewers that we have spoken to over the years believe that they can accurately gauge a candidate simply by speaking to them. From our experience, nothing could be further from the truth. Interviewing is less about "informal chats" and much more about gathering signals. A signal is a concrete indicator that tells you something about the candidate's suitability for the role. Therefore, the first step that leaders should take is to ask themselves (i) what signals they should be looking for, (ii) whether the current interview process allows for the gathering of these signals.

It is important to remember that signals can be both positive and negative. An example of a negative signal might be disinterest, expressed by asking overly generic questions. In order to be able to gather such a signal, your interview process must actually allow for time to ask questions. While this may seem obvious, it often is not so in practice: Many interviewers only allow for 5 minutes in the end to ask questions, a timeframe that is hardly big enough to gauge a candidate's true level of interest in the company.

Tip 2: Make Your Process Known Beforehand

It is important that the candidates know what to expect from your process even before applying, how long the process is supposed to be, details on each step and how long does it take to move between the different steps once they are completed. That way candidates can better plan their time and know upfront if they are willing to do what it takes to get into the company, in addition to that it helps keep the process more reasonable otherwise it won't attract the desired people.

Tip 3: Understand Staffing Requirements

Those closest to the ground tend to know best what resources are needed to turn roadmaps into reality. Leaders should gather feedback from engineers and managers in order to define staffing plans.

Tip 4: Define Attractive Compensation and Benefits That Reflect Market Realities (and Review It Periodically)

Although this is self-evident, we are surprised by how many leaders fail to understand that software engineers are expensive. Especially since the beginning of the COVID pandemic, demand has sky-rocketed and so has compensation. As with everything else, you get what you pay for. Companies that are still stuck in an "outsourcing" mindset will eventually fall behind as they naturally fail to compete in a global marketplace. Therefore, it is crucial to understand the positions that you are hiring for and define a suitably attractive compensation. At the same time, the company needs to keep a constant eye on the market to ensure that the values offered for the engineers that are already on the team remain attractive enough to mitigate their chance of leaving.

Tip 5: Recruiter Screening

Recruiters act as the first line of defense, identifying suitable candidates and screening as many bad fits as possible. Technical interviews are especially time intensive and costly, and therefore your initial screening should be as accurate as possible, bringing as many **suitable** candidates into the next round while eliminating the unsuitable ones. In order to achieve a high level of efficiency, you should

1. Provide recruiters with an accurate list of keywords to scan for.

2. Use years of experience/years in the market as a filter. Hiring recent college graduates for remote positions can be difficult and should be avoided. Instead, University career fairs or other forms of direct contact with Universities tend to be more effective.

Tip 6: Scheduling

Avoid scheduling back-to-back interviews and meetings. A golden rule of interviews is to (i) always allow 15 minutes for the candidate to ask questions, and (ii) avoid hard stops so that you do not need to cut the interview short if you can avoid it.

Tip 7: Tooling

Make explicit the tools the candidate is expected to have installed or prepared before the interview so they don't spend time setting them up during the interview. If accounts on specific platforms are required send the invites a few days earlier and ensure they have access to such platforms before the interview starts.

Tip 8: Hiring Scoreboard

The hiring scoreboard, also called interview rubric or interview matrix, is a tool that defines relevant competences that should be measured for a certain position during the interview. With it the person (or team) conducting the hiring process can attribute numbers within a given range (0 to 5 for example) to certain characteristics that they believe are relevant for the job. Having that numerical measurement allows an easier comparison between two candidates, an aspect that is usually highly subjective.

There are many templates online for this but it is important to note that the attributes, technical or not, that go into the scoreboard need to be defined by the interviewers. This process helps identify what is actually relevant for the job and also is useful while making the interview by guiding the interviewer on what to assess from the candidate.

One very important point when creating a hiring scoreboard, specially when there is more than one person involved in the hiring process, is to describe the scale that will be used to measure a competence and detail what constitutes each level of that scale. Example: When measuring the "technical knowledge on technology X" for a Senior Software Engineer position we can use:

* 0 – Never heard of it

* 1 – Studied a similar technology

* 2 – Has experience with similar technology

* 3 – Has superficial experience with it

* 4 – Has extensive experience with it

* 5 – Expert

The scale and what each number means will vary per competence but it is better to keep it always 0 = undesirable and 5 = perfect so at the end of the process we can sum the values and use it as a metric to compare candidates.

One last useful aspect of the scoreboard is that it can be used for giving feedback to a candidate that was not approved, by having numerical values for relevant characteristics you can provide useful insight on what the candidate can improve for their future.

Tip 9: Technical Screening

Technical interviews should answer the following three questions:

1. Does the candidate have sufficient technical knowledge for the job?

2. What is the candidate's true level of experience? A candidate with 5 years of experience on the CV might in reality only have 1 year of experience, repeated five times.

3. Does the candidate have the necessary soft skills to execute their job?

While behavioral interviews assess the candidate's culture fit, good technical interviews are structured in such a way as to allow the interviewer to gather some signals about the candidate's personality and what it would be like to work with the person.

One hour is usually too short to allow the interviewer to collect a sufficient number of signals to answer these questions with any level of certainty. A good approach is to apply one of the following three options to your technical interview process.

Option 1: Three Phases, Remote

Phase 1: A challenging take-home exercise that the candidate completes in their own time. The exercise is to be submitted using a version control system, and will be reviewed by the interviewing engineer(s).

Phase 2: Candidates that pass phase I will be invited to a I-hour technical interview, broken down as follows:

- 0 to 10 minutes: Introduction and Overview. Ask the candidate to give you a 1–2 minute overview of their background, and to confirm the role to which they are applying to. This serves as (i) an ice-breaker and low-ball question to ease any nerves, (ii) for the interviewer to confirm that they are interviewing for the correct role. Next, provide the candidate with an overview of what will happen during the upcoming hour.

- Until minute 30: Ask the candidate to share their screen and walk you through their implementation of the take-home exercise. This will allow the candidate to talk through any additional concepts and solutions that they did not tackle (but are aware of) and allow the interviewer to dive into the solution in detail, gathering signals that indicate that (i) the candidate did indeed complete the exercise themselves, (ii) has the sufficient technical understanding to dive deeper than just the demonstrated code. The key activity for the interviewer here is to ask technical questions.

- Minute 30 until 45: Ask general technical questions that are not related to the solution itself, but that help you gather further signals. For example, *"How would you go about testing this code?,""How would you ensure a high level of code quality when working with a team of engineers on this exercise?"* or *"What is your experience with <insert relevant framework/language/etc.>?"*

- Minute 45 until 60: Leave the floor open to the candidate. It is now their turn to ask questions

Phase 3: A I-hour long systems design question. The benefit of a systems design interview question is that it allows for more accurate gauging of a candidate's experience, since answers are not restricted to specific technical solutions/implementations. Instead, they involved bigger picture decisions, evaluations of all aspects involved in engineering, as well as requiring candidates to potentially make design decisions which are difficult to revert if they were implemented (and hence require careful consideration). Since system design interview questions are more open-ended, they can end up taking many shapes and forms and hence allow for a more collaborative setting. This in turn allows the interviewer to gather signals on what it would be like to work with the person.

Option 2: Three Phases, Remote

Phase 1: A 75-minute long technical screening consisting of a programming challenge which the candidate needs to solve while sharing their screen, thinking out loud as they do so. The interview is structured similarly to phase 2 in option 1:

0 to 10 minutes: Introduction and Overview. Ask the candidate to give you a 1–2 minute overview of their background, and to confirm the role to which they are applying to. This serves as (i) an ice-breaker and low-ball question to ease any nerves, (ii) for the interviewer to confirm that they are interviewing for the correct role. Next, provide the candidate with an overview of what will happen during the upcoming hour.

Until minute 45: Ask the candidate to share their screen and explain the exercise to them. Encourage candidates to think out loud, and emphasize the focus on arriving at a solution (rather than on implementing minute technical details). Candidates may feel pressured due to "having somebody watch over their shoulder," so do your best to make them feel at ease, and remove any hard stoppers (i.e., allow for the interview to run over the time limit if need be). The objective behind the programming challenge is to gather signals on (i) the candidate's ability to reason, abstract, solve and communicate; (ii) technical competence; (iii) behavior in a collaborative setting.

Minute 45 to 60: Ask questions regarding their solutions. Can they identify any problems with their code/solution? Are they able to think of an alternative approach? How would they test their code?

Minute 60 to 75: Leave the floor open to the candidate. It is now their turn to ask questions.

Phase 2: A 1-hour long systems design question. See option 1, phase 3.

Phase 3: Interview with an engineering manager or technical lead, designed to drill into any specific competencies that the position requires, but that could not be covered by phases 1 and 2.

Option 3: Three Phases, Two Remote, One in Person

Phase 1: A 75 minute long technical screening consisting of a programming challenge which the candidate needs to solve while sharing their screen, thinking out loud as they do so. This phase is identical to phase 1 in option 2.

Phase 2: A 1-hour long systems design question. See option 1 or 2, phase 2.

Phase 3: A day-long on-site, consisting of multiple rounds of interviews, including

- A collaborative programming challenge that simulates a typical work day at the company
- Interview with an engineering manager or technical lead
- Interview with stakeholders

The more time and interactions interviewers have with a candidate, the more signals they can gather. Hence, the more accurate their evaluation of the candidate will be. If a company can muster the necessary expenses and resources for on-site or in-person interviews, then it should do so. In-person interviews are a great way to get to know the candidate(s), and in turn allows them to more closely evaluate the company too. It also signals that the company is willing to invest in attracting good talent.

Conclusion

Everybody knows that, if you want your company to grow, you need to hire good professionals. However, many people forget that hiring is not just about growth: it is also about retention and maintaining a solid baseline. A few bad hires can destroy entire teams. To complicate things further, finding good talent is difficult. As such, we outlined a set of attributes that will help you hire the right candidates. In summary, these are humility, experience, a high degree of self-consciousness, technical ability, good analytical and good technical skills as well as the ability to anticipate problems before they happen.

Quality

If you put good apples into a bad situation, you'll get bad apples.

—Philip G. Zimbardo

In the previous chapter, we discussed the importance of hiring good engineers and how to find them. Furthermore, we outlined the attributes of good and bad software engineers, and gave practical tips on how to identify them. Now it is time to talk about how you ensure that your good hires do good, quality work. That is, we will discuss how to create a quality-centric environment that allows people to execute to the best of their abilities.

Broken Window Theory

In 1969, Philip Zimbardo (who became famous through his "Stanford Prison Experiment") parked two abandoned cars in two very different neighborhoods: one in a high-crime area (the Bronx, New York City) and the other in a low-crime, high-income area (Palo Alto, California). The car parked in the Bronx was soon vandalized and all items of value were taken from it. The car parked in Palo Alto however remained untouched for days, until Philip Zimbardo came back and smashed its window. Not long after that, the car was vandalized further.

Zimbardo concluded from this experiment that in areas where crime is commonplace, the community takes acts of robbery and vandalism for granted and hence accelerates bad behavior due to lack of concern. In low-crime

B. Jakobus et al., *Leadership Paradigms for Remote Agile Development*,
https://doi.org/10.1007/978-1-4842-8719-4_5

communities however, where such behavior is rare, the very fact that this behavior is rare and not visible acts as an inhibitor to antisocial behavior as people either feel some sense of accountability or believe that they will be held accountable.

In 1982 social scientist George L. Kelling used these findings as the basis of his "Broken Windows" theory:[1]

"Consider a building with a few broken windows. If the windows are not repaired, the tendency is for vandals to break a few more windows. Eventually, they may even break into the building, and if it's unoccupied, perhaps become squatters or light fires inside."

"Or consider a pavement. Some litter accumulates. Soon, more litter accumulates. Eventually, people even start leaving bags of refuse from take-out restaurants there or even break into cars."

In other words, the Broken Window Theory tells us that people will feel less bad for further breaking an already broken environment. Within the context of this book, the damaged environment might not be physical, but the lesson to be taken from Kelling and Zimbardo still holds: If you place good professionals into a dysfunctional environment, they are most likely to contribute further to its decline.[2]

Take your project's codebase as an example: When you start working with a new codebase that is already bad and broken, you probably won't feel bad for introducing further garbage (read: "quick hacks that we will address 'later'"). After all, the "codebase is already broken and would need to be re-written from scratch." On the other hand, when you start working with a new, tidy, well-designed, codebase you are much less likely to introduce new garbage on purpose. There is a psychological factor that inhibits you from adding garbage on purpose as you would be "the only guy pooping in the park."

If you do not want your project to fail, it is therefore crucial to pay attention to your work environment from the start. As a leader, you need to set high standards. Communicate clearly that code quality and operational security are a priority and ensure that the right processes are in place to control them. Invest in the necessary tools and frameworks that allow your team to meet these high standards. Encourage doers and tackle bad behavior head on. Inspire collaboration and discourage politics. Remember: *a general lack of concern will only breed further lack of concern.*

If you are wondering where to start when trying to increase the code quality on a project you are part of, consider the data shown in Figure 5-1.

---

[1] "Broken Windows: The police and neighborhood safety", The Atlantic, 1982
[2] We are not the first to associate Broken Window theory and software engineering. A blog post published in 2005 on codinghorror.com discusses the association in detail. https://blog.codinghorror.com/the-broken-window-theory/

What is the number #1 thing a company can do to improve code quality?

Code Review	24%
Unit Testing	20%
Integration Testing	11%
Continuous Integration	11%
Functional Testing	9%
Detailed Requirements	9%
Training/On-Boarding	4%
User Stories	3%
Static Analysis	3%
Demo Days	1%

n = 856

Figure 5-1. Results of a survey conducted by SmartBear on how to best improve code quality. Code Review and Unit Testing ranked at the top, whilst demos and static analysis were considered to have little effect. Source: "Take on Code Quality Early and Often," SmartBear, https://smartbear.com/solutions/code-quality/, visited 31/10/2022

Saying that we need to maintain a healthy working environment is all good and dandy. Most of us intuitively know when we work in a broken, toxic environment. But how can we define an unhealthy working environment concisely? What can leaders watch out for? What are the signs that an environment is "broken"? As with most things in life, there is never one concrete thing that we can point at and say *"Hey, this is why the environment is broken."* Instead, it is an accumulation of a lot of small things. The German philosopher Arthur Schopenhauer spoke about how our life resembles *"pictures in a rough mosaic; they are ineffective from close up, and have to be viewed from a distance if they are to seem beautiful."*

This is how one should think about the workplaces too: Lots of little things accumulate to form a bigger picture. Joe not responding to a message is just one small tile in the mosaic, and it may not be a big deal in itself. Similarly, one meeting not resulting in something actionable is just another piece and may not be a problem. But if Joe, and Jane, and Billy all do not respond to messages, if all meetings drag into inaction, if nothing really works and all interactions feel cold and lifeless; if all initiatives sink to the bottom of the sea and all features are buggy and broken, then the mosaic is one portraying a broken workplace. So in order to identify whether your environment needs fixing, step back from the day-to-day occurrences and try to see the big picture.

Slow Down

The previous section highlighted the need for setting high standards and maintaining a good quality codebase. One crucial ingredient for the latter is speed. Or, more importantly, the lack of speed. This cannot be emphasized enough. Slower is faster. Once you overload your engineer's plates, they will rush to complete their work. Rushing results in technical debt and bugs. By slowing down you allow developers to produce quality solutions that will stand the test of time and do not need to be constantly revised. Time allows people to think things through, discuss and explore new ideas and approaches. It allows problems to be identified before they happen.

Furthermore, it is important to note that even one person rushing and pushing for speed (when it is not necessary) can drag the rest of the team down as they need to review code and spot mistakes that could easily be avoided. That is, other engineers need to sacrifice their dev time to review code that is not up to standard.

A lot of needless rushing can be avoided by correctly managing deadlines. That is, by not treating soft deadlines as hard deadlines, understanding when deadlines can and cannot be changed, and by not using deadlines as a motivational tool.

Trust and Autonomy

We already discussed the need for autonomy in Chapter 3: Management; however, given how crucial it is to maintain a healthy work environment, we thought it prudent to reiterate: Once you hire the right people, you need to trust them to do their job (within reason).

Creating an atmosphere in which you do not trust your team, in which you second-guess every decision, will result in poor job performance and demoralize engineers over the long term.

It is counter-productive to hire smart, motivated professionals and then ask them not to think and act with autonomy.

1. You can supervise without breathing down everybody's neck.

2. You can trust yet still verify.

3. Putting processes in place to vet ideas/decisions, discuss solutions and verify and validate approaches is important.

It does **not** mean that you do not trust your people. Validating ideas is crucial to successful execution and is also a great tool to share knowledge among the team. Trust does not mean letting people loose without any accountability.

Trust between coworkers is also essential for a highly functional team, it impacts motivation, collaboration, stress levels, and even willingness to stay in the company. Especially in remote environments. The lack of direct contact, or being in different time zones should not be an excuse, but yet another incentive to increase trust and autonomy.

Below we list a few actionable items that can be used to create an environment that promotes trust:

- Listen to people, discuss their ideas and test them when suitable. Hearing and nodding is not enough, managers need to experiment with the ideas given to them otherwise, employees will create expectations that are never met.

- Provide autonomy for people to make their own decisions. This one is obvious, but an important aspect is how the company deals when an employee makes a mistake. If the company does not offer proper support or does not stimulate some risk-taking, the supposed autonomy is not real.

- Share important information with your employees. It is easy and convenient to share positive information but having a consistent way of sharing both positive and negative information makes the employees know that nothing relevant will be hidden from them.

In Chapter 10, we take a deeper dive into Trust and how to specifically create a remote environment that promotes it.

Hierarchy

As Roger V. Gould details eloquently in his book *Collision of Wills: How Ambiguity About Social Rank Breeds Conflict*, "*the primary source of conflict in our society is the attempt of one person to achieve dominance over another without substantive reason.*" Gould's main argument is that this striving for dominance is not the result of our position in the social hierarchy (or our want to attain a higher position), but instead is due to our uncertainty of our position. That is, people enter into conflict with each other because they do not know where they stand. Once people know what their position is, what their responsibilities are, and where the boundaries lie, they feel safe and hence are less driven to try and exert their dominance over others.

Establishing a clear-cut hierarchy does not imply placing people on golden pedestals. Nor does it mean putting a rigid structure in place (people should remain accessible). One title does not make one person better than another—

every title and position carries weight and importance. Instead, having an explicit hierarchy means that everybody's role is clearly defined. We can all continue being in the same boat while also knowing what it is we are expected to be doing. As William Pleahy said: *"the hierarchy should not fear what we are doing."*

Sometimes people confuse hierarchies with titles. That is, they confuse a tool with the end goal.

Like a hammer alone does not make a house, a title alone does not create hierarchies. Hierarchies are about defining clear boundaries, and a title is one of many tools that can help you establish such boundaries.

Clear responsibilities, goals, and expectations must be explicitly defined to avoid confusion and conflict. This helps the person in the given position and their coworkers, and the company. For that, whenever possible, have a written down description of the role, its responsibilities, do's and don'ts, and how this role relates to its peers, that's accessible by everyone.

Competent professionals that operate in an environment with clear boundaries operate more efficiently and effectively as they

1. Know exactly who is responsible for what. Who to contact, who to inform, and where the ball stops rolling.

2. Take the initiative as it is clear who is to be held accountable for the initiatives.

3. Avoid stepping on toes and walking on eggshells (which in itself is time-consuming and demoralizing and contributes to creating a broken window environment).

Processes

Anybody who has ever built a house knows that construction is done in phases and that each phase consists of a series of precise processes, starting with the planning phase, during which the architect sits down with the client and figures out exactly what to build. The size of the house, the number of rooms, the location, the number of bathrooms, the size and layout of the kitchen, etc.

Once all of these pieces of information have been systematically gathered, the architect begins to iteratively draw the plants. From there onwards, the engineer becomes involved, structural calculations are put down on paper and verified, 3D models are being constructed, planning permissions obtained, and so on and so forth. Only once the initial phase is complete do the actual phases of construction begin: rock breaking, leveling…. Only from there on will the foundation be built.

Now imagine building a house without any processes in place. Rock breaking starts before the building permission has been obtained. Parts of the foundation are built as the architect still finalizes the plants. The structural calculation is being worked on as the builders start laying the bricks on a partially completed foundation. Would you want to live in such a house? We wouldn't because the necessary processes that help guarantee the structural integrity of the building, and hence our safety, were not in place.

If we look at the fast range of variables, requirements, moving pieces, interconnected systems, and dependency hierarchies of any software system, we quickly come to realize that many pieces of software are far more complex than even the tallest of buildings. Yet, the importance of having processes in place when building such software is often overlooked (while it is almost taken for granted when it comes to the construction of physical objects).

When leaders put strong, solid processes in place, they essentially create structures to avoid a "broken window environment," as processes allow people to

- Plan more accurately and hence manage expectations
- Ensure quality control
- Build trust (i.e., we know that for X to move into stage B, stage A will need to have been completed successfully. For stage A to be completed, we know that criteria 1, 2, and 3 will have to have been met)
- Validate and verify decisions
- Track progress
- Identify problems more quickly and accurately
- Build hierarchies
- Know who owns certain tasks

But what exactly does that mean? The phrases above—*"putting a process in place," "ensuring quality control,"* and *"plan more accurately"* all sound very abstract.

How *exactly* do processes help with job execution? Well, at its core, a process defines how to do something. It provides a framework, or outline, for executing a set of steps. That is, processes define an initial state and a clear outcome as well as guidance on reaching the end state given the initial state. Take interviewing candidates as an example: At the beginning of the interview process, we have a candidate of whom we don't know much. By following a specific set of steps—(i) reviewing the CV, (ii) initial screening call, (iii) 1-hour technical interview, (iv) 1-hour systems design interview, etc.—we arrive at a set of signals that tell us whether a candidate is suitable for the given role. By reviewing how many candidates are at what stage of the interview process, we get an idea of the overall progress of our recruiting initiatives, and can, in turn, use this to plan upcoming roadmaps as we can more accurately forecast to what extent our staffing requirements will be met.

In other words, by having an interview process in place, we can track progress and plan around it. Expanding further, we can easily see how an interview process can also help ensure quality control. For example, by specifying the exact criteria that a candidate must meet to pass each phase of the process (rubric), and maintaining scorecards, we can more easily identify and filter out unsuitable job candidates while also establishing a baseline for a company that, in turn, helps build a certain level of trust.

We used both construction and interviews as illustrations, as they are obvious examples of processes that most of us are familiar with. Without needing to be a builder, engineer, or HR professional, we more or less know what interviews or construction involves. That makes it easy to formulate as a process.

Conversely, if you do not know how something is done, it is very difficult to formulate the activity as a process. Or, as W. Edwards Deming put it: *"If you can't describe what you are doing as a process, you don't know what you're doing."*

A rather obvious duh moment, right? Unfortunately, many companies do not consider this obvious at all. Countless companies use processes defined by people that do not have the faintest idea about their underlying activities. Therefore, beware of those that try to create processes for activities that they themselves have never performed.

Good Processes

As illustrated in Figure 5-2, when establishing processes, leaders should be aware of the following characteristics that are exhibited by "good" processes:

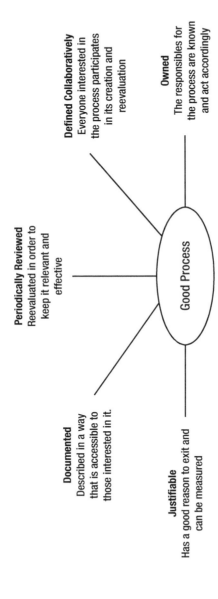

Figure 5-2. Good processes are documented, defined, and owned collaboratively, justifiable, and periodically reviewed

Justifiable

By being justifiable, processes have a good reason to exist. In other words, it is possible to demonstrate that the process helps with some objective or metric. It is critical that the process's effectiveness can be objectively measured. In the few cases where the improvements are subjective, and no explicit measurements can be done, one should strive for checking the progress more frequently and do a "temperature check"—a simple thumbs up/down with most of the people involved.

A process is meant to solve or avoid a problem from happening. Finding the facts which clearly indicate that the core problem is being addressed helps to justify the existence of the project in its current incarnation, or serves as a trigger for a process review—more on that later.

Documented

Documented processes are described in an accessible way, allowing people unfamiliar with them to understand and execute the process correctly.

Try adopting the practices of versioning your process so you can share the learning with people getting involved with the process after it's been running for a while.

People, with good reason, might question why a process works "like this" and not "like that." Keeping historical records of previous discussions, decisions, attempts, and improvements. This can both save time and avoid the stress of constantly reviewing certain core topics.

Periodically Reviewed

Circumstances change, and the initial motivations for a process might no longer exist, making the process obsolete or unnecessary.

Similarly, a change in context or operating environment might require the processes to be amended or improved. Therefore, it is crucial to review and, where necessary, revise established processes regularly.

It is important to note that process review and adaptation is also a key aspect of the agile methodology, as iteration facilitates continuous improvement by incorporating new knowledge. It helps keep the mindset of treating the process as a project: kickstart w/ group, break into milestones, break each milestone into tasks, deliver each milestone, and have retrospective about it, deem it done.

Along the same lines, it helps if you roll out your process gradually to those people who will be affected by it. Just like you're rolling out a feature to your users: first target 10%, then 25%, then 50%, then 100%. This way, you can learn and course-correct before impacting everyone and increase the overall confidence in its effectiveness.

Note that while improvement is the objective, experimentation is the way to achieve an improvement. Of course, one possible output of experimentation is failure. In this context, failure means that the process is either ineffective in achieving its goals or unnecessarily complicated (hence decreasing the team's performance).

A good process can accommodate the experimentation and potential failure because

- Aside from being justifiable, it is also measurable. This means that we can compare objectively or subjectively whether the process works as intended. All the stakeholders should make comparisons and evaluations, so we can ensure every part has a voice.

- As it is documented, we can quickly identify what changed between the different versions of the process, helping the identification of problematic changes.

Another form of review is **feedback**. Allowing for extemporaneous forms for triggering process review can help avoid going too long executing something that might not make sense anymore.

Make sure that everyone involved has a channel to express opinions on the current state of things and that the person driving the process can start a discussion around an aspect of the process or the process as a whole.

Defined Collaboratively

Processes should not be defined in a top-down manner. Instead, they should be the creative effort of all stakeholders. A process defined without the participation of the people expected to be impacted by it runs the risk of focusing only on the output and ignoring relevant steps on how to achieve that.

Furthermore, processes that are defined in a top-down manner also won't impart a sense of ownership. By allowing the people impacted to have a voice and input on the process development, you make it more likely that they'll follow it and help with improvements over time and may also encourage experimentation as failures are shared among the group, rather than pinned on an individual's sleeve.

On the other hand, a process that is created bottom-up might focus too much on how to execute it and lose sight of some steps that are important to managers.

Balance, as with most things in life, is key here.

Ownership

It is vital for the successful execution of a process to clearly define the expectations around roles and responsibilities of those in charge of maintaining, enforcing, and periodically reviewing the process. Known as "process owners," these individuals should have the necessary autonomy while also being responsible for effectively collaborating with stakeholders.

Note that part of the process owners' duties is to avoid processes getting stalled (e.g., due to ineffective decision making or uncertainty around responsibilities). To aid with the latter, we recommend the adoption of a decision-making framework such as DACI. By using a decision-making framework, process owners can clearly define who-does-what in such a way that new leanings can be incorporated quickly and effectively.

Bad Processes

Bad processes are not just the inverse of good processes described in the previous section. Why? Let's consider process ownership as an example: It is still possible for a process that is not defined collaboratively to effectively achieve its goals. Similarly, an undocumented process can't be considered a "bad" process simply because it isn't documented.

Instead, what we consider "bad" processes are processes that actively harm productivity. Bad processes are a weight around people's ankles. Processes that do not solve a problem but exist for the sake of existing. They are overkill. They are an end in themselves, and being imprisoned by them is extremely toxic to a company as a whole. We most likely have experienced such a "bad" process, and spotting them is not difficult. Therefore, we won't dwell too much on the topic aside from highlighting that one of the most effective ways of spotting and eliminating bad processes is by simply asking yourself what the process is trying to solve and then checking whether the process is actually solving it. If you cannot apply some form of measurement or metric to the given process, you immediately know that the process is problematic. The next step is to gather feedback on the process. As already discussed, processes should be defined collaboratively and are not meant to be owned by one single individual. Ask those directly affected by the processes what they think of it and whether they believe the process to be beneficial.

Conclusion

Once you hire the right people, you need to provide them an environment in which they can execute to the best of their abilities. This means

1. Establishing a clear hierarchy. When people know exactly what their responsibilities are and where boundaries lie, you minimize the potential for conflict.

2. Trusting people and giving them the autonomy to do their job. It is counter-productive to hire smart, motivated professionals and then ask them not to think or act on their own.

3. Setting high standards for your product, maintain a good, solid codebase, and give people the tools they need. Maintaining high standards means knowing how to manage deadlines and avoiding creating an environment in which people need to constantly rush. Slower is faster.

4. Setting clear boundaries.

5. Creating processes.

Once you have established a healthy, functioning working environment, you need to maintain it. That is, you need to work to keep it healthy and functioning. Just like a window with broken windows, a broken, uncared for environment, breeds carelessness. Remember: If you place good professionals into a dysfunctional environment, they are most likely to contribute further to its decline.

Feedback

Continuous improvement is better than delayed perfection.

—Mark Twain

Feedback is one of the most powerful tools for facilitating improvement, both within an organization and in our lives as a whole. Defined as *"the transmission of evaluative or corrective information about an action, event, or process to the original or controlling source,"*[1] feedback evaluates the outcome of our actions or behavior, telling us whether what we did was "good" or "bad," "successful," or "unsuccessful." To appreciate just how powerful and widespread a tool it is, imagine for an instance, life without feedback: Consider speaking to a friend, family member, or colleague who is cold as ice, who shows no reaction whatsoever. We have probably all encountered such a person before, and found interacting with them difficult on many levels. Now imagine if everybody you encountered were like this. Combine this with the lack of in-built feedback mechanisms in tools and systems that we use every day. Entering a wrong password, or filling out a form incorrectly prompts the system we use to do nothing. Zilch, no error message, no popup dialogs. Pressing the unlock button on our car keys invokes no noise or no blinking lights to indicate that the car was successfully unlocked. When giving a presentation at work, everybody just stares blankly ahead without giving any indication of whether or not they are listening.

---

[1] Merriam-Webster, www.merriam-webster.com/dictionary/feedback

© Benjamin Jakobus, Pedro Henrique Lobato Sena, Claudio Souza 2022
B. Jakobus et al., *Leadership Paradigms for Remote Agile Development*,
https://doi.org/10.1007/978-1-4842-8719-4_6

Feedback is such an ingrained part of our lives, that we probably have never considered the above scenario before. Instead, many people tend to associate the term itself with the dry forms and HR processions that managers go through every 6 months or so. Rarely do we appreciate how feedback allows us to lead richer lives. But feedback can also be a dangerous tool if used incorrectly. Again, let's perform a little thought experiment to illustrate this: instead of imagining a world without feedback, envisage one in which feedback is given at complete random. Entering a password randomly results in an error dialog informing you that the password is incorrect, even when it isn't. Your car sometimes beeps, sometimes doesn't when unlocking it. Your friends randomly laugh at you as you confess a personal, serious issue you are having. How would such a world make you feel? How would you be able to navigate, and grow within it?

Applying the above thought experiments to the context of this book, we see why feedback is such a crucial, yet also dangerous, element to success, and why in Chapter 1, we said that mastering it is one of the essential nine pillars for successful leadership. In this chapter, we are going to discuss how to use this great resource properly, avoiding common pitfalls.

Characteristics of Good Feedback

Now that we toyed with the idea of what living in a world without feedback, or with improper feedback, would feel like, we have gained at least some appreciation of the importance of feedback itself.

Before we can move on to discussing how best to give as well as ask for feedback, we should first understand the characteristics of good and bad feedback. In essence, good feedback is (i) specific, (ii) relevant, (iii) given in public only when positive, (iv) participative, and (v) well-thought through and well-planned. Feedback that does not check the aforementioned five boxes is usually dangerous and destructive, and should be avoided.

Let's talk about the five characteristics of good feedback in detail.

Specific

When giving feedback, ensure you have specific instances of the observed behavior to mention, generic comments that can't be linked to particular events are counter-productive and might be easily dismissed with some examples where said behavior didn't happen. For instance, *"In our last planning session you were not very participative, we were hoping to hear your thoughts"* is preferred over *"You are too quiet in the meetings."*

Being specific is also important when suggesting what needs to be improved. While it is easy to criticize someone's actions, an important part of the feedback is showing a different way to act. Having an action plan with concrete steps on eliminating or mitigating the undesired behavior can be of great help.

Relevant

Feedback should always be relevant to the given task, topic, or operating environment at hand. When you attempt to authenticate with incorrect credentials, the application processing the login provides you with the feedback that the login attempt was unsuccessful. It does not present you with an irrelevant error message from 3 days ago. Similarly, any feedback you give to coworkers should be relevant to their job performance. Sure, it sometimes is tempting to provide general guidance, life or career advice to others, but when unsolicited, such feedback is poorly spent: It is likely to make you look like a know-it-all, and does not help others perform their jobs more effectively. Instead, limit feedback to what is relevant. Explain the real impact of the behavior and how relevant that consequence is. Keep in mind that oftentimes the person incurring a certain behavior does not have a clear idea of the impact associated with it. *"Due to your nonparticipation in the last planning session we didn't allocate time to setup the infrastructure that we assumed was completed, this will delay the deadline in a week impacting other projects"* instead of *"Your nonparticipation will impact the deadline and cause a delay."*

Private or Public

This is certainly the most straightforward rule: Praise in public, criticize in private. When you criticize in public the person being criticized will automatically assume a defensive position making it almost impossible for the message, no matter how correct and relevant it is, to be understood and internalized. Not only that but the person feels that her image is also being attacked which might escalate into unnecessary conflict.

Participative

Don't make the feedback a monologue that reinforces a top-down relationship. Instead, stimulate the participation of the other person by asking whether they agree with your assessments or not, what would they do differently if they had the chance, and what made them choose that particular action. Unlike when using software, feedback is a two-way street. Especially negative feedback should be open to discussion: the world is a complex place, and sometimes actions and words are misunderstood. Furthermore, with people we only ever see the tip of the iceberg: There is a depth to us all, and many motivations and justifications invisible to the observer.

Regular

Providing feedback should be part of the company's culture as one important way to stimulate continuous improvement. As part of a process, it should happen regularly. At the same time, we don't need to always wait for the periodic meeting in order to give feedback, as long as the main requirements listed above are respected.

There are different tools for making feedback regular, like 1-on-1 meetings, annual reviews, etc. If it happens too often, like weekly or biweekly, those meetings might not have enough content to be discussed, converting them into time sinks. On the other hand, if you provide feedback just once per year you are not creating the **continuous** improvement that is expected from it. A good rule of thumb is that if, as part of their annual or bi-annual review, the person is surprised about the feedback they receive, then their manager has not been doing their job. Of course, it is up to the individual leaders to decide the cadency of the feedback. Sometimes this cadency can vary from team to team, from person to person. Don't worry if it takes some experimentation to get it right. Just remember to make feedback constant. As Adam Grant eloquently put it: *"Good managers don't wait for formal meetings to help you grow. They make it a daily priority. The sooner you get feedback, the sooner you can break bad habits and learn better ones."*

Planned

In order to satisfy the aforementioned requirements, planning is required. You need to gather evidence to support your claims, anticipate some potential responses from the person that is receiving the feedback and put yourself in the other person's shoes. How would you react if you were the one receiving such feedback? What exactly are you solving for, and does the gathered feedback help create the desired solution or outcome?

It is also a good idea to check your motives when planning to give feedback. Are you giving the feedback in order to make yourself feel better or to check a box in your career growth list? Or are you trying to actively solve a problem or help/motivate others to grow? If you answered *yes* to the former, then it is best to refrain from giving feedback. Remember: the purpose of feedback is to generate improvement by changing a particular behavior. It is not supposed to be a tool to vent, harshly criticize, or gratuitously offend the other person.

Characteristics of Bad Feedback

We define "bad" feedback as feedback that is damaging. Damaging to the goal at hand, damaging to the interpersonal relationships across your team, and/or damaging to the company as a whole. Of course, just as was the case with the "bad engineer" checklist some chapters ago, bad feedback isn't just the inverse of good feedback. That is, when inverting the characteristics of good feedback discussed in the previous sections, we don't automatically get damaging feedback. For example, feedback that is irregular doesn't necessarily affect the relationship between the giver and receiver of the feedback. Similarly, unplanned feedback might not damage the operating environment—it might simply be useless. Void of meaning. At the same time, bad feedback isn't any less damaging because it is *planned* (and hence shares a characteristic of good feedback).

Instead, bad feedback fails to solve the problem at hand, is not actionable, and harms the relationship between the giver and receiver.

No matter how it is given, it tends to share the following characteristics:

- **Personal** – That is, it is not objective feedback, and is given for personal reasons, mainly to boost the giver's image. Oftentimes, personal feedback is coupled with the inverse of a characteristic of good feedback: it is negative feedback that is given in public.

- **Offensive** on some level. It may not be due to language or format, but it hurts, offends, or puts the receiver down in some shape or form.

- **Unproductive** in that it does not help the receiver, is sufficiently general to not be actionable, and does not solve any problem at hand

- **Negative** in nature. Positive feedback is rarely damaging. Feedback that is negative however can demotivate people and destroy relationships if not relevant, actionable, or framed in a productive manner.

Remember: good feedback is used to help the other person grow, while bad feedback is used to satisfy a need for whoever gives it, being inherently unhelpful to the receiver.

How to Ask for Feedback

Not all companies have a culture of providing regular, planned feedback. However, that shouldn't stop you from directly asking for it when you think it could be of benefit to you. Effective leaders should always use feedback as a tool to make sure that they are not blindsided.

The first step when asking for feedback is to identify people that have enough information about your work to craft useful feedback. Ideally your direct boss/manager, some of your peers, or even clients. Once identified, make sure that you trust the person: If you believe they are not willing to help you it is preferable to search for someone else. Next, prepare a small set of questions to ask. The emphasis here is on "*small*": providing feedback when you request it, should not be very time consuming to others, so don't occupy their day with a 10-page questionnaire. Everybody is busy, and, by answering your questions, the responder is taking time out of their day to do you a favor. When creating your questions, create a mix of both single/multiple choice questions and open-ended questions that you'd like them to respond to. Last but not least, remember that all questions should be about your work. Nobody cares about your hairstyle.

Lastly, if asking in person (as opposed to async), ensure that you give some time for the person to really reflect about your work. You should also be prepared to ask follow-up questions once you receive the feedback, focus on suggestions that might be too generic or not actionable. Try to really drill down on what action could lead to the result which that person would expect.

Below are three template questions that solicit a useful set of information. You should, of course, adopt their phrasing to suit your context, and make the responses anonymous in order to raise the level of comfort of those responding (if you are in a higher position relative to the responder):

- **How would you rate <insert name> overall job performance over the past 6 months?** *Present this question with a fixed scale, for example of 1-5.*

- **List 3 positive aspects of <insert name>'s work. What did <insert name> do particularly well?**

- **List 3 negative aspects of <insert name>'s work. What could <insert name> have done better? What concrete steps could <insert name> do to perform better?**

Acting on Feedback

Receiving feedback is the easy part. The hard part is acting on it. That is, becoming a better person/colleague/worker. There is only so much advice that we can give: ultimately, it is up to you to take on board what other people have to say, and work on yourself. What exactly "working on yourself" involves, largely is up to the individual. There is no size to fit all. However, based on our experience, people that drastically improve their behavior and performance over time, all share five distinct characteristics. We will touch briefly on each in the following sections, but in summary, high performers (i) have strong emotional self-control, (ii) are planners, and (iii) know how to validate their behavior, (iv) respond to feedback in a timeline manner, (v) are self-aware. Furthermore, strong performers act both on positive and negative feedback. A natural tendency of many people is to relax after they do something well, and only focus on improving their weak points. However, being good at something means actively maintaining skills, and consistently holding yourself to high standards. As such, strong performers use positive feedback as a form of positive reinforcement: praise drives and motivates them to continue excelling at what they are doing well.

Don't Take It Personally

Dismissing or minimizing a criticism is a very natural reaction when we are on the receiving end of it; however, in a professional context, we need to be more cautious. First, it is important to understand that a given feedback is meant to help us improve, and second, that the target of the feedback is not ourselves or our image (things we'll fight fiercely to defend) but instead a very specific action or behavior that needs correction. Therefore, the first step toward improvement involves emotional self-control: don't take constructive criticism personally.

Have a Plan

If the person that provided you the feedback read this book they probably gave you some actionable suggestions on how to improve, if not it is up to you to come up with a plan to adjust the specific behavior. Don't be afraid to reach out to the person giving the feedback for help.

Validate the New Behavior

With a plan in hand it is time to execute. There are situations where it is preferable to validate the plan itself first, in cases where the stakes are higher, otherwise you can just try the new approach and ask the person that gave you the feedback if that looks adequate now.

Respond in a Timeline Manner

Responding to negative feedback in a timely manner, and showing that you are committed to improving is crucial for maintaining trust and preserving your image. This does not mean that you are expected to resolve your weaknesses all at once. Instead, it means making and showing progress. Colleagues that are not committed to acting on feedback will cause resentment and distrust. Furthermore, they will eventually lose their sources for feedback (and hence a valuable source for improvement) as those that provide them with feedback are unlikely to continue "wasting" their time providing it if they see that the receiver is unwilling to accept and respond to it.

Self-Awareness

Self-aware people have a clearer understanding of themselves, know what they what and where they stand, this allows them to respond better to negative feedback as they have an easier time identifying the root cause of the undesired behavior. At the same time it is easier for them to incorporate changes that they believe are aligned with their long-term objectives

Words of Caution

Now that we know what good and bad feedback looks like, how to ask, and how to react to it, it is time for some brief words of caution: if a lot of feedback is available to you, pick your battles carefully. All of our actions and choices incur a cost, and if you stop and act on everything, you risk creating a lot of change. That is, you are at risk of kicking up dust which can irritate others or make it difficult for others to accomplish their work. If acting on a feedback item would result in big changes, determine what the general consensus is first: Are you hearing this feedback from only one individual? Or is this feedback common? Does everybody/the majority believe that the given change should be implemented?

Effective 1:1s

One-on-one (1:1) meetings are regular meetings between a manager and their team member, with the purpose of (i) building a trusting relationship between both parties, (ii) allowing the manager to help the team member to perform well consistently, (iii) preparing for performance review, and (iv) providing a safe space for the team member to raise concerns with their superior. We would like to stress that the above purposes are all equally important and somewhat intertwined. In short, 1:1s play an important role in the feedback process (of course, they also play an important role outside of this process: they are much more than feedback channels, and can be very varied in style and substance. But discussing these nuances is beyond the scope of this book). If either party comes out of the meeting feeling:

- Unable to **express themselves** openly or clearly
- Unable to **ask for help, raise concerns,** or (to a healthy extent) vent
- Unable to **establish a personal relationship**

…then something is wrong and the 1:1 meeting is unproductive.

Furthermore, in order for *any* meeting to be fruitful, the parties must come prepared. In theory, the same applies to these 1:1 meetings, but in practice this rule is often ignored due to the informal nature of these meetings. Ensure that you do not fall into the trap of the latter, and that in-between meetings, both parties

- Keep notes of achievements, blockers, frustrations, and suggestions

- Complete any outstanding action items

- Come prepared to answer the common and important question (such as what needs to be done (by either party) to attain a promotion)

It is also important to note that, when providing feedback as part of a one-on-one meeting, that both parties are best served by a limited focus: avoid discussing more than two issues (ideally both issues should be related). Any more than that, and one risks

- Making the receiver of the feedback feel attacked (in the case of negative feedback), or overwhelmed in the case of general feedback

- Diluting the conversation, resulting in a general discussion rather than one that produces distinct action items

Remember: one-on-one meetings are two-way streets. On the one hand, they allow the manager to evaluate and help the team member. On the other hand, they create a close personal relationship, allowing the team member to provide feedback, and hence helping both parties keep a pulse on things.

Effective Listening

The sad truth is that most of us are not natural-born listeners. Listening is a skill, and as with any skill, it requires practice. Therefore, chances are, you won't become a better listener simply by reading a book. You will, however, be able to gather some useful tips and knowledge that you can apply in reality. These include

- Listening actively rather than passively by taking notes, and maintaining focus.

- Asking follow-up questions and engaging in the conversation. If the person doing the talking feels that they are speaking against a silent wall, they will eventually stop giving information.

- Caring about the topic at hand. As a leader, part of your job tasks involve dealing with people. Just like with any other task, you can only do the task of listening well if you care about it.

- Starting every conversation on the premise that the other person knows something that you do not know. Everybody has something to teach you. Always remain conscious of the fact that we sometimes naturally view conversations as competitions, and counteract this tendency when you see it surfacing. Remember: you are here to listen, not to compete. Or as the stoic Epictetus once put it: *"We have two ears and one mouth so that we can listen twice as much as we speak."*

- Be curious and genuine.

- Reflecting on what is being said. Avoid jumping to a new topic immediately and remember that communication is often more about what is not being said than what is being said.

- Repeating or paraphrasing what the speaker said. This gives the speaker a break to reflect, and gives them the necessary pause to think of additional things to say on the topic. It also promotes "active listening" on behalf of the listener, improving your memory of the conversation, and allowing the listener to gather their own thoughts and reflect on what is being said.

- Using the power of silence when appropriate. That is: ask a question, then let the other person speak. Then remain silent—don't immediately jump to a conclusion and start blabbering. Remaining silent will cause the other person to continue talking.

- Relaxing. As with any task, we perform worse at it if stressed.

The Power of Labels

Maybe the famous quote *"great people make you feel that you, too, can become great"* is rooted in labeling theory. That is, the theory that the people's behavior is (in part) determined by what others think of them, because the "self" is the product of social interactions. How others interact with us, and what they think of us, creates and shapes how we see ourselves. Jón Gunnar Bernburg summarized this notion concisely in the *Handbook on Crime and Deviance* (pp.187–207):[2]

---

[2] Handbook on Crime and Deviance by Marvin D. Krohn (Editor), Alan J. Lizotte (Editor), Gina Penly Hall, ISBN-10: 9781461412106

> [Labeling] theory assumes that although deviant behavior can initially stem from various causes and conditions, once individuals have been labeled or defined as deviants, they often face new problems that stem from the reactions of self and others to negative stereotypes (stigma) that are attached to the deviant label (Becker, 1963; Lemert, 1967). These problems in turn can increase the likelihood of deviant and criminal behavior becoming stable and chronic. In the words of Lemert (1967), deviant behavior can become "means of defense, attack, or adaptation" (p. 17) to the problems created by deviant labeling. Thus, being labeled or defined by others as a criminal offender may trigger processes that tend to reinforce or stabilize involvement in crime and deviance, net of the behavioral pattern and the social and psychological conditions that existed prior to labeling.

Although labeling theory is primarily viewed through the lens of criminology, there is an argument to be made that it also holds true in the modern workplace. If we consistently label a good employee as an underperformer, chances are that they will eventually underperform—be it due to lack of motivation or because they give up hope of ever casting off this label in the current workplace—turning our opinion of them into a self-fulfilling prophecy. Many times the "labels" we apply to our colleagues are automatic and not something we actively think about: a wrong answer shows that one is not technically competent or inattentive; joining a call late means that one is careless and irresponsible and so on.

What we can learn from labeling theory in these situations is that we should be cautious in making judgments too soon—and to realize when we are making them. How we feel about others affects how we interact with them, which in turn affects our relationship with them and possibly their work performance as a whole.

Unless an employee shows obvious and repetitive signs of underperforming, leaders should therefore be especially cognizant of how they view and label their subordinates. Instead of immediately labeling employees and colleagues, good leaders maintain self-control and focus on the positive aspects that each person brings to the table (note: this does *not* mean that obvious bad apples should not be dealt with swiftly). When translating this into concrete actionable items, focusing on the positive means

1. Framing critical feedback in a positive light, as well as considering the other's strengths when judging their weaknesses

2. Recognizing other people's work via shout-outs in public chat rooms or meetings or thanking people in person

3. Actively encouraging people during 1:1 sessions

4. Never publicly blaming or shaming someone

5. Keeping performance reviews positive, framing criticism as forms of helping the other person advance their career, and using strong criticism only when a concrete problem needs to be resolved

Conclusion

Feedback is an incredibly powerful tool, and as any powerful tool, when used incorrectly the damage it creates can be significant. The purpose of this chapter was to serve as a manual for correctly applying this tool. In short, we learned that, in order for us to be able to unleash the power of feedback, it needs to be (i) relevant, (ii) specific, (iii) regular, (iv) planned, and (v) participative. The giver of feedback also needs to be empathic enough to be able to distinguish when the feedback should be given in public or private. Negative feedback given in private as part of one-to-one meetings should be limited: The giver should focus on no more than two topics at hand, lest the receiver feels attacked or leaves the meeting demotivated. Both participants of feedback meetings should come prepared: action items should have been completed and questions prepared ahead of time. Questions raised with the objective of *receiving* feedback should be short and concise, with at least one open-ended component. Most importantly however, they should only ever be asked to persons that the receiver trusts. Last but not least, the receiver should always act on feedback in a timeline manner (failing to do so risks drying up your sources of feedback and will likely generate resentment and distrust), which in turn requires you to *not* take the feedback personally. Keep in mind that dismissing or minimizing a criticism is a very natural reaction when we are on the receiving end of it; however, it is important to understand that the giver of the feedback is trying to help us improve (they are not questioning ourselves or attacking our image). After all, that is what feedback is all about.

Managing Expectations

Expectations were like fine pottery. The harder you held them, the more likely they were to crack.

—Brandom Sanderson, The Way of Kings

Our expectations deeply affect how we interact with other people. In the working environment where we often depend on other people in order to complete our own work, this becomes even more apparent. When we set high expectations and they are not met we get frustrated and disappointed. What makes us create expectations that are unlikely to be met? How should we best deal with unrealistic expectations? How are expectations formed? We will try to answer these questions in this chapter.

How Expectations Are Formed

Expectations are beliefs we form on how the future should be. They help us plan for the future by allocating scarce resources (like time, money, and energy) on activities that might yield the results we desire, and are formed based on the information we have available at the moment as well as based on our experience from past events. Once we get used to a certain pattern that

© Benjamin Jakobus, Pedro Henrique Lobato Sena, Claudio Souza 2022
B. Jakobus et al., *Leadership Paradigms for Remote Agile Development*,
https://doi.org/10.1007/978-1-4842-8719-4_7

is repeated over time, we develop an expectation that the same action or event should repeat itself again in the future. This is normal human behavior and can be observed in many creatures across the animal kingdom as well. Any dog owner knows that whenever they get the leash their dog will act excitedly, expecting to be taken for a walk.

In the working environment, we create expectations all the time as well: on how coworkers would react to a certain demand, how customers will react to a new policy or service and what the boss will do if an important deadline is not met. We create expectations so often that it is common to not carefully assess whether they are realistic or not, many times we assume that because a behavior has always happened in a certain way it will continue to be repeated as such in the future. This is called inductive reasoning, or induction, and has been a subject of philosophical discussion since 300 BC when Aristotle first started pondering it, but as any experienced stock trader can assure you: Past behavior is not a guarantee for future behavior.

Sometimes we unintentionally create false expectations simply by agreeing with people when we shouldn't: A manager that says *"It would be nice if we could deliver this before the end of the quarter, do you think that is possible?"* is not directly asking for a commitment, but depending on the answer given, it might become one. While *"I'm not sure, that date seems a bit tight considering the other demands we have"* makes it clear that you are not committing, on the other hand by saying *"Yes, we have other demands but we probably can do that"* you do create an expectation that might haunt you in the future. Notice how it was said that it *"probably can be done,"* when negotiating or even simply communicating this type of content it is specially important to be completely clear and avoid ambiguity at all costs. Otherwise, each side will interpret what was said according to what is most convenient to them.

Unrealistic Expectations

Unrealistic expectations[1] are those that are very *unlikely* to be met and that can be identified as such at least by part of the team responsible for setting and/or executing it. Many realistic expectations are also not met due to other factors, like external events (recession, change in customer behavior) or unpredictable forces (like a pandemic). These are subjects for entire books in their own right, and outside the scope of this chapter. In the following sections, we will only cover *unrealistic* expectations and how they impact the working environment.

---

[1] Note that this should not be confused with *misaligned expectations* which are usually an easily addressable communication problem and have much lower impact overall.

Origin

Neuroscientists, psychologists, biologists, and sociologists have spent decades (if not millennia) trying to explain the inner workings of the brain, and how we make and form decisions and expectations. Stripping away complex and biological factors, we can try and simplify existing literature on the topic and condense it into a nutshell format that we hope is of practical use to our subject matter at hand. As such, based on our experience, the most common factors involved in the formation of unrealistic expectations are

- **Misaligned interests**: Some manager or boss needs to force the team to a deadline that is unfeasible because that would grant them some benefits, like a raise, a bonus, or prestige.

- **Insufficient or incorrect information**: When expectations are based using incorrect variables their result won't be correct, understanding what is relevant for any given artifact is a prerequisite to define a reasonable expectation.

- **Incompetence**: Some people simply don't deliver and try to postpone the inevitable outcome as much as possible, pushing the deadlines whenever they can in a continuous manner.

- **Biases**: As already discussed in Chapter 3, our brains have limited processing power, and as a result we tend to form biases to help us navigate a complex and uncertain world. This results in disproportionate weight in favor of or against an idea, thing, or person, leading to the formation of expectations that are simply highly unlikely to be met.

- **Lack of Situational Awareness**: In its simplest form, Situation Awareness (SA) means *"knowing what is going on around you."*[2] While SA has its roots in the aviation industry, and goes back to pilots in WWI, it applies to any environment and is a fancy way of determining how apt an individual is at perceiving and comprehending their environment and then processing this information. Specifically, it tries to determine *"how people pick and choose information, weave it together, and interpret it in an on-going and ever-changing fashion as both situations and operator goal states change."*[2] Formulated less rigorously

---

[2] Situation Awareness Analysis and Measurement", ISBN 0-8058-2134-1

and put into the context of this chapter:: when you know what is going on around you, you can manage expectations. Leaders that do not know what is going on around them, tend to create unrealistic expectations.

It should be noted that, in some sense, the above items intertwine: Incompetence and biases, for example, are closely related and may be caused by incorrect information. Similarly, insufficient information can be a cause for poor SA (although the opposite—too much information—can be a cause too). We leave it up to the reader to untangle these relationships: a good exercise, and a difficult task in reality. The important thing is to be aware of these factors: once you recognize them for what they are, you stand a chance of counteracting them.

It should also be noted that, in some ways, expectations can be situational. There are a number of factors that can lead to misalignment that is not inherent to the individual but created by transient events, like someone having bad information or going for a bad breakup. One must be careful not to diagnose and label the nature and reason of unmet expectations without enough context.

Examples

Unrealistic expectations come in many shapes and sizes. Within the world of engineering however, they are most commonly manifested in the form of unrealistic deadlines, scope creep, and unmatched autonomy. We will discuss each of these in turn below.

Unfeasible Deadlines

Unfeasible deadlines are the most common type of unrealistic expectations, delivery dates that can't be achieved with the existing resources are forced on a team that usually needs to select a path they'd prefer to avoid if possible, like working overtime, cut important features (i.e., removing scope), or incur into technical debt that hopefully will be addressed one day.

Such deadlines usually happen in a top-down manner, that is, a manager/boss decides the date with little to no input from the team and simply communicates to the team that it must be met. However, that is not always the case, sometimes team members are overconfident or ignore important aspects of the tasks, assuming they are more of what they are already used to and say that it is possible in a timeframe that is not realistic.

Scope Creep

Scope creep happens when *unexpected* features or demands are added to a project that simply was not ready for them. A project that was properly scoped and had a reasonable deadline might start to receive new requests that break the previously agreed terms, this is what we classify as scope creep.

Conditions that affect the project might change suddenly and the need to adapt is a force that should not be ignored, but embraced, however, this is no excuse to ignore any previously defined plan and work in a chaotic manner, disregarding previous effort in favor of information that might be previously known but ignored. Teams should have a clear mechanism to identify which tasks bring higher value to the company at the lowest possible cost and prioritize them.

Unmatched Autonomy

Unmatched autonomy happens when an individual expects a certain level of autonomy, usually on a new position or on a new project, and is faced with a different reality: red tape or excessive bureaucracy that simply does not allow them to make the choices they thought possible before, like a team leader that expected to be able to choose the people that would join their team or which technologies to use.

Although there are other manifestations of unrealistic expectations, like megalomaniac missions, unfeasible performance, or unmatchable precision for AI-based estimation, the three we listed above are the ones we see happening more often and tend to be independent of the sector the organization is in.

The Impacts of Unrealistic Expectations

Unmatched expectations affect everyone inside an organization and its products, services, and even customers.

At the individual level, a lot of pressure due to some unfeasible deadline might cause stress and demotivation. In case that is something recurrent, it can lead to turnover or even burnout.

Inside a team, it might manifest in different forms, like morale erosion as people will feel that their best is never enough, loss of confidence in cases where different teams need to interact and one (or both) of them never deliver on the expected timeframe (even though such timeframe is impossible). Ultimately, it might lead to a culture change where the company's *modus operandi* is based on such expectations and everyone knows they are expected to work long shifts and sacrifice scope or quality in order to meet impossible targets. Once that culture takes place, people realize that planning sessions lose their meaning because reasonable deadlines won't be respected anyways or the scope will grow making them irrelevant.

Lastly, it also impacts the company's services and products, when deadlines and scope cannot be changed what suffers is quality. In software projects, this means not only more bugs but also bugs that take longer to get fixed, are more likely to return some time after "fixed" and have a more widespread impact throughout the system. Tech debt is another side-effect when quality is sacrificed, if not paid it piles up and makes even simple changes harder to achieve and riskier to do.

How to Deal with Unrealistic Expectations

By far the most important tool to avoid unrealistic expectations is communication. Clear, non-ambiguous communication. It is the onus of the task doer to ensure that he makes his opinion known about the reasonability of what is being asked, to consider all the information available and decide whether it is feasible or not. When we omit ourselves, be it for fear of what others might think of us, be it because we believe we'll be ignored, we are accomplices and signatories of that bad decision. Unsurprisingly that omission will come to haunt us down the line.

We know this is easier said than done but most people tend to think that saying "no" is actually much worse than what it is in reality. A responsible company that trusts its hiring process will assume that their internal teams are composed of competent and professional people, such people are able to have diverging opinions and discuss it in a non-confrontational manner, exposing the arguments that those opinions are based on, ensuring the premises that lead to such ideas hold true. Assuming you did your homework when you expose the reasoning behind a disagreement or explain why a certain deadline isn't realistic an honest and reasonable person will understand and together you can search for a better arrangement that satisfies what is needed.

Once agreements have been reached it is time to document them. Written commitments are another important tool to deal with unrealistic expectations. We tend to believe that once a decision has been made it will remain unchanged indefinitely, that is rarely the case. In cases like scope creep, having written documentation about what exactly was agreed upon is essential to ensure that in case new demands get added people know that the agreed deadline is not accounting for it, so accommodations need to be made. Here, we are not necessarily talking about a specific document just for this purpose; ideally, we should rely on tools we are already using and just ensure that people use the same source of information as "the source of truth." A sprint with X items and 50 points allocated to it can very well serve for this purpose for instance.

Aligning Expectations

Unrealistic expectations aside, another significant source of frustration in software development, are poorly aligned expectations.

The most common example of expectation alignment involves the engineering manager helping product managers, and stakeholders to know *if* a feature is possible and *when* it can be implemented. At the same time, the team needs to know what they will be working on and the given timelines. Everybody involved needs to be able to plan around this. This is where a good manager shines. That is, it is the manager's job to set expectations and to align them with all involved parties. When doing so, make sure you:

1. **Understand** what the stakeholders expect and validate these expectations with the team to ensure that these are technically feasible.

2. **Prioritize** features that have the lowest cost and highest impact on the business.

3. **Ensure that the team understands** the main goals of a project and why it is important to the company.

4. Try to **anticipate** obstacles before they occur(so they can be removed or mitigated) by checking in with both the team and the broader circle of stakeholders.

It is important to note that once your team understands what is required, they will automatically be able to help you calibrate expectations. Engineers may suggest paths that can help you achieve the objectives—for example, by illustrating features that might seem expansive to a nontechnical person but are not.

Although project-related expectations are arguably the most visible and highest repercussion, they're by no means the only kind that a manager needs to handle.

Other types of expectations, while not as visible, are equally important and should be done with the same tact, for example:

- Visibility of sensitive or confidential topics while keeping the team informed

- Promotions and raises

- Organizational structure changes

- Process changes

- Technology changes

- Cultural behavior

While not comprehensive, we hope that this list illustrates how expectation setting is a critical aspect of the life of a manager, how diverse and time-consuming it can be, and how impactful the consequences can be when not properly handled.

Conclusion

Expectations are part of our personal and professional lives. We form them all the time as they are convenient tools used to plan the future. A large portion of these expectations, we formed subconsciously. Some are the subject of biases or extrapolations of past experiences. Others are based on subtle signals that we don't perceive consciously. Especially within a professional setting, this can be dangerous. After all, our brains have a limited capacity, and we are apt at "bending" our perceptions. We have no way of telling how much of what we perceive to be real, actually is. Psychologist Lee Brosnan calls this "naive realism," or as Arthur Schopenhauer puts it: *"every man takes the limits of his own field of vision for the limits of the world."* While to a certain extent, there is very little that we can do about this, we should reflect on this regularly. Especially when we feel that our expectations are not being met.

We should also try to identify and mitigate (as soon as possible) *unrealistic expectations*. That is those expectations that are known upfront to be unfeasible or near impossible. Unrealistic expectations come in different shapes and forms. Sometimes they come from the top, and we need to make sure our opinions and concerns about them are heard. Other times, we create them ourselves inadvertently. and care with details is essential to avoid these latter traps. Regardless of how they are formed or where they come from, it is important to remember that once we start to accept unrealistic expectations as part of the company culture individuals, teams and the product and services the company provides will suffer.

Bureaucracy

Bureaucrats derive their power from their position in the structure, not from their relations with the people they are supposed to serve. The people are not masters of the bureaucracy, but its clients.

— Alan Keyes

To understand how profoundly bureaucrats shaped modern human existence, we need to travel back in time to the end of the last ice age (11,000 B.C.), which saw the dawn of a new era. It was then that humans began slowly settling down, leaving behind their scattered hunter-gather existence, in exchange for a more sedentary lifestyle. Across Eurasia and Africa, farming, herding, mining, and metallurgy led to massive increases in population size, eventually turning small tribes into large, complex, political organizations (such as kingdoms). This increase in complexity required the rise of two powerful new technologies: writing and abstract thought. While archaeologists suggest that the small groups that composed early hunter-gatherers had relatively limited mathematical capabilities that usually did not exceed counting past 10, larger groups of people are more difficult to coordinate, and hence require more complex ways of accounting and spreading ideas. The Babylonians and Egyptians, who are among the early pioneers of mathematics and writing, developed advanced numeric systems as well as methods for multiplication, solving equations, and working with fractions which, among other things, they applied to advancing construction and taxation. The latter allowed these ancient civilizations to amass great wealth, turning them into flourishing empires.

© Benjamin Jakobus, Pedro Henrique Lobato Sena, Claudio Souza 2022
B. Jakobus et al., *Leadership Paradigms for Remote Agile Development*,
https://doi.org/10.1007/978-1-4842-8719-4_8

How is this relevant to managing agile projects? Well, regardless of what ancient civilization we look at—from Babylon to Rome—we see that record keeping was at the heart of their complex political organization. The administration of their vast empires would not be possible without it, as the establishment of accountability, as well as the formulation, regulation, and communication of information and activities, is what allowed for coordination and hence expansion and complex organization in the first place.

These fundamental activities of documentation and coordination were undertaken by specialists, whom we today refer to as "bureaucrats" and who, unfortunately, often have a bad reputation. The word *"bureaucrats"* itself is a derivation from French and translates to *"government by people at desks"*[1]—a notion that is accurate, albeit hints at a problematic, distanced, and inefficient form of government. It is important to remember then, as we talk about bureaucracy throughout this chapter, that this *"desk governance"* forms the fabric of our society. As such, we consider bureaucracy to be the fundamental building block for coordination, and once you realize this, you also realize that most things that we know of today would not be possible without it: Just like bureaucrats built ancient empires, they build modern ones—be it political ones like the US or Chinese governments, or business empires—like those run by Jeff Bezos or Tim Cook.

But just like a building block gives a building its form, it can also be the cause for collapse if stacked unevenly, too high, or without the support of steel and cement. This is the central message that we are trying to convey in this chapter, and if you stop reading now, then you already know most of what we are about to elaborate on: Bureaucracy in itself is an essential force that acts as the lifeblood of any sizable business. Too much of it, however, will stifle and eventually kill productivity.

Types of Bureaucracy

For the purpose of this book, we are going to split bureaucracy into two segments:

- **External**: Bureaucracy that we do not control and simply need to conform to, government imposed processes like tax declarations, ISO certifications, SEC registration statements, privacy policies, vendor agreements, or company bylaws.

---

[1] Merriam-Webster Dictionary, www.merriam-webster.com/dictionary/bureaucrat

- **Internal**: Bureaucracy is defined within a company and that the company itself has autonomy to change. Examples include Product Requirements Document (PRD), Request for Comments (RFC), and Objectives and Key Results (OKR) documents.

As external bureaucracy is (for the most part) outside of an organization's control, this chapter is solemnly concerned with *internal* bureaucracy. Unless specifically stated, assume that any reference to bureaucracy refers to the latter.

From Process to Bureaucracy

As we discussed in Chapter 5, processes define clear steps and requirements on how to achieve certain objectives. Over time, as our operating environment changes, these processes need to adapt and incorporate mechanisms to remain useful (or be replaced altogether). As changes accumulate, the complexity of processes tends to grow, which affects the number of required actions to complete them (i.e., processes grow and require more effort to both maintain and execute. An increase in bureaucracy tends to result in an increase in total effort expended to accomplish a goal). The latter typically refers to the amount of the "inputs" or information it needs. That is, when processes evolve and grow, they increase the amount of required paperwork. In other words, they become more expensive and time intensive. Ideally, processes should remain malleable and adaptive so they can continue to be relevant and evolve to deal with new scenarios. However, unless this particular aspect is properly cared for, what we see is the "solidification" of processes, where they become less malleable over time and stop re-evaluating the necessity of all its requirements resulting in what we actually perceive as unneeded bureaucracy.

In general, it is advisable to be careful when judging processes. Processes often have hidden depths, and upon first seeing a process, we tend not to be aware of all scenarios that the process is capable of dealing with. A process that demands a lot of information that might seem unnecessary at a first glance has possibly faced a situation where that information was needed before but (at the time) was not available. This hidden depth might affect the adopter's perception and make the person assume that a given process is simply unneeded bureaucracy when in fact there is a lot of complexity that is simply not visible to the naked eye.

That said, the fact that a certain process demands a lot of energy or information from its adopters is not always a sign that it is extremely capable and ready to deal with different situations. Just as any other product of human action, it might be poorly optimized or a victim of misaligned interests.

A poorly optimized bureaucratic process would be one that although it might cover a lot of different scenarios, many of those scenarios are unlikely, overestimated, or even totally outdated, despite that, the user needs to comply with a long or time-consuming list of requirements just to avoid those unlikely scenarios. Like one of your meetings that could easily be an email, although simple and apparently innocuous they tend to happen often, killing the team productivity without delivering the expected result.

A bureaucratic process with misaligned interests however can be very damaging to the organization, those types of processes can be qualified as such when the person controlling/executing the process wants to shift the burden of his work onto the adopter of the process or wants to prevent certain objectives from being accomplished in the first place. One common example of such conflict of interest in engineering often occurs between the verticals within that department. For example, when dividing teams into separate units of backend and frontend rather than full-stack units that act in cohesion, the interests between these two units may conflict. One common approach for conflicting teams to "get their way" and work on what *they* consider a priority (but which may not be a priority for the company as a whole) is to introduce roadblocks in the form of paperwork. Instead of collaborating with the team requesting a certain feature or implementation, they first require this team to jump through as many hoops and approval processes as possible: unnecessary RFCs that take a long time to review, duplicate PRDs that may require approval from other sectors of the organization, and so on so forth. Instead of cooperating coherently and transparently, different teams create paperwork as shields to protect their own interests.

Internal Organization

The larger an organization, the more people and activities there are to coordinate. Seeing how the latter (organization of key activities) is the key objective of bureaucracy, the bureaucracy system of an organization naturally grows as the organization increases in size.

More people also naturally implies more interests, and as the number of distinct individual interests grows, so do the chances for malalignment. In other words, damaging bureaucratic processes that arise due to conflict of interests may increase exponentially to the amount of new hires (each new person leads to a n*n-1 new set of relationships.). It is important to understand that this does not *need* to be the case if a company (i) pays careful attention to its internal organization, (ii) instills a culture of collaboration rather than competition, and (iii) gives autonomy to teams to allow them to make decisions without, or with minimal, external dependencies. Based on our experience, the former is the most important to get right, as even if a company's culture may not be universal across the organization as a whole, organizing people effectively allows the company to remedy cultural shortcomings.

Effective organization in essence means creating groups of people that share a common interest that aligns with the interests of the company as a whole. Vertical vs. horizontal organization provides a good example of this. Engineering departments that are organized in verticals have a top-down command structure where responsibilities are "sliced" by technical capability. For example, a backend team is controlled by a director and subordinates on one hand, and a frontend team is controlled by a different director and subordinates on the other hand. A horizontal organization is a synonym for worker autonomy and, within our context, involves creating full-stack teams that all take ownership of certain products or parts of products. In the case of the full-stack team, interests are aligned: Their objective is the success of the team, and hence the product as a whole. In the case of the vertical teams, cohesion does not come so naturally: faced with one product, two teams essentially compete to achieve objectives set forth by different directors. If the vision, philosophy, or approach to the engineering of these directors differ in any way, conflict is likely to arise as a result. As such, preventing misaligned interests is much more difficult with vertical organizations as leadership needs to always be closely aligned in order for the machine to function well.

Another example of misalignment, now on a strategic level, is the incorrect use of Key Performance Indicators (KPIs) and Objectives and Key Results (OKRs). Companies use these as tools to set the goals that will lead them to reach strategic objectives but often fall into the trap of setting too many of them on vertical instead of horizontal levels. An example of this is team-level OKRs. Although there's nothing inherently wrong with the practice, they're often set in a way that discourages collaboration. Every team wants and is accountable for achieving its goals, but if the goals are not set correctly or aligned with those of other teams, groups will actively avoid helping each other because they have their own urgencies.

Verticals also bring with them a natural increase in process work: Different teams need to coordinate, and coordination naturally means some form of bureaucracy.

Inefficiencies

Today, a large body of research and literature exists examining the relationship between organizational size and bureaucracy. One indicator of the level of bureaucracy within an organization is to use what is called "administrative intensity." That is, *the number of managers, professionals, and clerical workers divided by the number of craftsmen, operatives, and laborers employed by the organization.*"[2] When studying administrative intensity, researchers frequently reference two prevalent theories: Parkinson's Law and Public Choice Theory. The latter, when applied to bureaucratic processes, essentially argues that bureaucratic processes introduce inefficiencies as organizations grow. That is, *"economies of scale are eventually counter-acted by bureaucratic congestion."*[3] Similarly, Parkinson's Law *"states that bureaucracy grows regardless of the quantity of work to be undertaken and even when the overall size of an organization is shrinking" (Boyne 1986; Parkinson 1957).*[4] In other words, Parkinson's Law argues that bureaucracy is an animal in itself and not naturally coupled to productivity. Instead, bureaucratic processes can take on a life of their own, generating work and consuming resources for the sake of generating work and consuming resources. Bureaucracy, proponents of Parkinson's Law argue, is an end in itself, not a means to the end of other activities.

Both arguments have merit, and indeed we have seen their real-world manifestations many times. For example, if you set a 1-hour meeting, people will fill up that hour and rarely try to finish it sooner. Bureaucracy does indeed increase with organization size and *can* become a burden as it does. Bureaucratic processes *can* also be carried out for the sake of it, without serving coordination or record keeping (although a certain number of bureaucrats may always be required due to external bureaucratic constraints, like laws or legal compliance due to industry regulations like PCI, HIPAA, etc.) With emphasis, the word *can* in the previous two sentences, as these inefficiencies don't' always need to hold true. They can be avoided by (i) understanding what problems internal bureaucratic processes should be solving, (ii) understanding what healthy bureaucracy looks like, (iii) identifying the attributes unhealthy bureaucracy exhibits, and (iv) knowing how to apply the understanding of bureaucracy in order to strike a balance and solve for inefficiencies. We will discuss each of these points in the following sections.

---

[2] Pondy, L. R. (1969). Effects of Size, Complexity, and Ownership on Administrative Intensity. *Administrative Science Quarterly, 14*(1), 47–60. https://doi.org/10.2307/2391361
[3] Pondy, L. R. (1969). Effects of Size, Complexity, and Ownership on Administrative Intensity. *Administrative Science Quarterly, 14*(1), 47–60. https://doi.org/10.2307/2391361
[4] Boyne, G. A., & Meier, K. J. (2013). Burdened by Bureaucracy? Determinants of Administrative Intensity in Public Organisations. *International Public Management Journal, 16*(2), 307-327. https://doi.org/10.1080/10967494.2013.817261

Characteristics of Healthy Bureaucracy

Just like ordinary processes, healthy bureaucracy, or healthy bureaucratic processes, share the following characteristics:

- **Justifiable** – They have a good reason to exist and that reason is still relevant today as it were when the process was created;

- **Periodically Reviewed** – People responsible for this process review it periodically in order to ensure that it is still relevant, making adjustments as needed. An important part of this revision process is to ensure that cases which were required in the past are still relevant today. Requirements that are now obsolete present opportunities to decrease the complexity of the process and should be abandoned.

- **Documented** – The required information, steps, and estimation time to complete are all relevant information that should be available on some common repository so people that need to go over this bureaucratic process may plan accordingly.

- **Malleable** – In order to avoid the "solidification" we described previously it is important to keep the process flexible enough to adapt to new scenarios while efficient to deal with the existing ones, this balance of course is not trivial, ensuring that all the involved stakeholders can present their views (usually during period reviews) is a good way to ensure that everyone is satisfied or at least understands the requirements for a heavier process.

Healthy bureaucratic processes are also usually self-evident: that is, their reason for existence is clear to all involved. When executing a healthy process, team members should not be asking themselves what the purpose of a given activity is. The activity should be a natural part of their job, not a hurdle or hoop that people jump through.

Characteristics of Excessive Bureaucracy

Excessive bureaucracy is much more than simply the absence of the characteristics exhibited by healthy bureaucratic processes. Instead, they share some or all of the following attributes:

- **Misaligned interests** – When the person responsible for the process does not have the same interests as the adopters of a process the end goal diverges from what it should be, resulting in unneeded overhead. Unnecessary meetings, paperwork that is written once and never read are the most common side effects.

- **Inertia** – The bureaucratic process exists for its own sake. That is, "is the way it is simply because it always was this way." The responsible for the process is not interested in making changes or the system that is in place does not support a change that would make it better. The side effects tend to be unneeded overhead just like with misaligned interests but the reason behind it is different.

- **MBA-Syndrome** – The creators of the process read somewhere that this bureaucratic process is what they should implement, without properly understanding *why* and *how*. They decided to copy procedures without really understanding what these procedures are intended to solve. As a result, the people executing the nonsensical process do not know why they are executing it. Nobody can provide a clear objective, nor does anybody know what problem the process is solving for.

Striking a Balance

Successful bureaucracy means striking a balance between productivity and record keeping. The best tip that we can give to this end is: use your common sense. If you don't know why you are performing a given bureaucratic process, if its activities are duplicated in some shape or form, or if executing the bureaucratic process impacts your productivity or timelines, then it's time to revisit (and probably discard) the entire process.

Furthermore, pay attention to your internal organization. How you structure teams and departments, and the egos that play a role in creating this structure, will have a big impact on whether or not "desk governance" forms a healthy part of your organization, or whether it drains resources.

Last but not least, remain vigilant. Just because a process that was created in the past made sense then, does not mean that it makes sense today. Review and revise. And do so periodically.

Conclusion

Staying true to the underlying message in this chapter that record keeping should be efficient, concise, sensical, and goal-oriented, we terminate this brief chapter abruptly. Ancient bureaucrats laid the foundations of our modern civilization. They ushered in the dawn of writing and abstract thought, casting our planet into a new bright light. It is up to our common sense to ensure that this light is not blocked by stacks of paper. Whether executing existing processes, or defining new ones, keep in mind that (i) a certain amount of record keeping is always required due to external bureaucratic requirements, (ii) misaligned interests, inertia, and "the unknown" are all characteristics of unhealthy processes. If your process exhibits any of the latter attributes, it's time to review and revise.

Ethics

"So you think that money is the root of all evil?" said Francisco d'Anconia. "Have you ever asked what is the root of money? Money is a tool of exchange, which can't exist unless there are goods produced and men able to produce them. Money is the material shape of the principle that men who wish to deal with one another must deal by trade and give value for value. Money is not the tool of the moochers, who claim your product by tears, or of the looters, who take it from you by force. Money is made possible only by the men who produce. Is this what you consider evil?"

—Ayn Rand

We could not write honestly about strategies for success without discussing ethics. Specifically, (i) the role that strong and weak ethical positions play in the success and failure of projects and companies, (ii) what the primary causes for weak ethical positions are, as well as (iii) their impacts and how to ensure a strong ethical position.

However before we embark on this journey, we want to emphasize that our discussion of ethics will be restricted to this chapter only, and therefore incomplete. Entire books have been dedicated to ethics, morality, good and evil, and all that we can do in this chapter is scratch the topic's surface.

With our disclaimer out of the way, we can now begin our chapter by introducing a polarizing figure: Ayn Rand. Hated and loved by many in the world of business, Ayn Rand shares a similar fate to that of Karl Marx (yes, we can already hear our readers gasp). Although Rand and Marx stand on the

© Benjamin Jakobus, Pedro Henrique Lobato Sena, Claudio Souza 2022
B. Jakobus et al., *Leadership Paradigms for Remote Agile Development*,
https://doi.org/10.1007/978-1-4842-8719-4_9

opposite sides of the philosophical and political spectrum, they both profoundly shaped the world we live in today, and proposed both brilliant and terrible ideas while becoming victims of their own success. Most people today associate Marx with his economic theories (communism) yet forget that he was also the father of sociology and raised valid criticisms of capitalism. Thanks to his ideas and writings, governments in Europe adopted social policies that helped many—even if the reason for their introduction was just to placate the communist parties at the time.

Similarly, today Ayn Rand is primarily associated with laissez-faire capitalism, her "glorification of the ego," her failure to accept that market forces cannot solve everything and that "productive achievement" is the ultimate goal of one's life. It is often forgotten (or purposefully overlooked) that she believed that people could and should pursue their own self-interest **without** sacrificing others (*"Man—every man—is an end in himself, not a means to the ends of others; he must live for his own sake, neither sacrificing himself to others nor sacrificing others to himself"*), and that the exchange of value should be fair. The latter notion she summarized through Francisco d'Anconia's famous money speech—quoted at the beginning of this chapter—in her seminal novel *Atlas Shrugged*, in which the character essentially states that money represents the fundamental idea of exchanging fair value for fair value, and only exists because of men who produce: *"money is the material shape of the principle that men who wish to deal with one another must deal by trade and give value for value."*

It is precisely the above quote that lies at the core of this chapter: the premise that when you build and sell something to others, then you should offer fair value for money. This means that the money you make should be made by offering a good product to your customers; and a good quality service to those buying your time. Unfortunately, many companies fall into the trap of making money otherwise—for example, by manipulating users into spending money, or by marketing something that has a net-negative value as something "positive" (more on this later). Similarly, to be able to build a valuable product, you need to offer fair value to those building it. In other words: pay them a fair wage, as opposed to outsourcing to digital sweatshops. And when you are the one being paid, you should perform your services to the best of your abilities, and put the interest of the one paying you ahead of your own for the period of payment. A failure to do so—that is, to exploit others, regardless of whether you are the worker or the company—is essentially what leads professionals down the slippery path toward a weak ethical position. Let's look at this path in detail…

The Lucifer Effect

We respect that many readers may have different personal, religious, or philosophical opinions on what moral or ethical behavior entails. In no way do we intend for our understanding and definition to be absolute. Nevertheless, for the purpose of a concise, focused discussion, we feel the need to establish a context within which to base our arguments and observations. Within the context of this chapter, we therefore adopt the definition proposed by the American neuroscientist and philosopher Sam Harris, who believes that moral/ethical behavior is any *"behavior that allow[s] people to flourish."*[1] It follows that unethical behavior is any that prevents the well-being of people, or as social psychologist Philip Zimbardo puts it: *"knowing better but doing worse."*[2] Why then, assuming that the majority of people generally know better, do people *"do worse"*? Why are the fraudulent acts and unethical behaviors committed by executives and employees of Nestle, Deutsche Bank, Wirecard, Enron, HSBC, Petrobras, and DuPont not singular occurrences, but instead feel like they are a constant thread winding itself through all levels of society? While this is a difficult question that much smarter authors than us have tried to study and answer for many years, at least some part of the answer can be found in our surroundings. We all like to think that we are special, the hard truth is that we are mostly the by-product of our environment, and that most of the time our highly held morals are mere pastimes that make us feel good about ourselves, but which we happily discard if they get in our way. *"Too often we look to the stars through the thick lens of personal invulnerability when we should also look down to the slippery slope beneath our feet"* is what Philip Zimbardo wrote in his 2007 book *The Lucifer Effect: Understanding How Good People Turn Evil*. In it, the author painstakingly details his famous "Stanford Prison Experiment," a milestone in social psychology which illustrated how situational forces can turn perfectly good people into immoral monsters. The essence of the experiment can be summarized as follows: Zimbardo and his research team created a simulated prison environment in order to study the effect that situational variables have on the behavior of individuals. To this end, they recruited a group of ordinary[3] people and divided them into two groups: prisoners and wardens. The wardens were given uniforms and free reign over the prisoners, with their sole objective being (i) maintaining order and (ii) preventing the prisoners from escaping. The crux of the experiment was that it quickly ran out of control and had to be cut short after only 5 days. It took Philip Zimbardo almost 40 years to digest his guilt of the horrors he caused, concluding that *"good people can be induced, seduced, and initiated into behaving in evil ways. They can also be led to act in irrational, stupid, self-destructive, antisocial, and mindless ways when they are immersed in "total situations" that impact human nature in ways that challenge our sense of the stability and consistency of individual personality, of character, and of morality."* He went on to state that his experiment showed how the *"subtle power of a host of situational variables*

---

[1] "The Moral Landscape", Sam Harris

[2] "The Lucifer Effect: Understanding How Good People Turn Evil", Philip Zimbardo, ISBN-10: 0812974441

[3] By ordinary we mean people that had no history of violent behavior, no criminal record or other exhibited any indicators that might have signaled a disposition to commit atrocities

can dominate an individual's will to resist. [...] We see how a range of research participants—other college student subjects and average citizen volunteers alike—have come to conform, comply, obey, and be readily seduced into doing things they could not imagine doing when they were outside those situational force fields. A set of dynamic psychological processes is outlined that can induce good people to do evil, among them deindividuation, obedience to authority, passivity in the face of threats, self-justification, and rationalization. Dehumanization is one of the central processes in the transformation of ordinary, normal people into indifferent or even wanton perpetrators of evil."

The Stanford Prison Experiment is central to this chapter, as it illustrates the importance of creating an environment in which our faults don't go unchecked. As soon as leaders fail to recognize the power of situational forces, and permit the formation of a climate which promotes the loss of personal identity, fails to protect individuals, and inhibits destructive behaviors, then they lay the groundwork for dishonesty, fraud, and violence (both physical and psychological). We will examine the most common paradigms that lead to such a setting in the following section.

Factors That Help Create Environment That Promotes Unethical Behavior

If the environment is so crucial at shaping our thoughts and actions, then what can we do to ensure that our work environment has a positive effect on people, rather than a negative one? A good starting point is to become aware of the primary factors that, in our opinion, create environments that promote unethical behavior.

1. The Number Games

Failing to focus on value and instead only focusing on metrics that drive business numbers is a symptom of poor ethics. High ethical standards mean developing a solution that you can stand over.

From our experience, one common factor that helps create environments which promote unethical behavior is an **obsession with metrics**. To understand what we mean by this, consider the following scenario: Leaders set out to build a product, and in order to do so, they need data points to know how their product is performing, how users use their product, and on what to base future decisions about the product. Especially in software, metrics is an important tool for building a good product. The problem arises once leaders lose sight of building a good product, and consider metrics as an end in themselves. Metrics should be a tool—one of many. Once leaders become obsessed with metrics, moving the needle becomes the key objective, and is placed above everything else. An ethically correct company earns money by providing value; not by driving metrics. And while the two can go hand-in-hand, they often do not. In fact, a purely metrics-focused approach to product development is almost always counter-productive to the product and business as a whole: Some metrics try to capture too much subjectivity, which in turn makes them less reliable/precise. Yet, a company where metrics is king often overlooks this, and therefore the actual value of the metric decreases considerably.

"If you can't measure it, you can't manage it." said Peter Drucker. However, in an attempt to measure subjective parts of the business, like customer satisfaction, team performance, and many others, leaders come up with some formulas that don't properly capture the depth of what they are trying to measure. Worse yet, more often than not, some composite subjective metrics are built, that is, subjective metrics that use other subjective metrics as part of their formula amplifying the inaccuracy mentioned before. At the same time, the *expectation* about the strength of these metrics becomes unrealistic, yet findings themselves are treated as decisive. Criminologists call this the "CSI Effect," and while the latter is a problem in courtrooms it also applies to business decisions. In essence, the "CSI Effect" phenomenon occurs due to our false understanding of data and data gathering, which consequently gives us a false sense of confidence. Dr. Dylan Evans describes this more eloquently in his book *Risk Intelligence*, when he writes: *"Science rarely proves anything conclusively. Rather, it gradually accumulates evidence that makes it more or less likely that a hypothesis is true. Yet in CSI and other shows like it, the evidence is often portrayed as decisive. When those who have watched such shows then serve on juries, the evidence in real-life court cases can appear rather disappointing in contrast. [...] In 2010, a study published in Forensic Science International found that prosecutors now have to spend time explaining to juries that investigators often fail to find evidence at a crime scene and hence that its absence in court is not conclusive proof of the defendant's innocence."*

We can rephrase Dr Evan's explanation to become more relevant to the context of software development: *Metrics that we gather, using tools such as Segment and Mixpanel, rarely prove anything conclusively. Rather, these tools can help us to gradually accumulate evidence that makes it more or less likely that a hypothesis is true. Yet, people with a false understanding of statistics, and science as a whole, often incorrectly interpret the gathered data as being decisive.*

This results in leaders drawing the wrong conclusions, and over time, creating a wrong vision of their environment as a whole as the decisions that they make, are based on information constructed from data points gathered using metrics that do not represent reality. Leaders that operate in a highly metrics-driven environment, therefore need to have at least a basic knowledge of data science. That is, they should understand how data gathering and analysis work at a fundamental level, and should be able to distinguish "good" data from "bad" data, as well as "bad" measurements from extraneous factors. Leaders that lack such an understanding, yet still act on metrics, should understand that they do so recklessly. Similarly to how one would not drive a car without having previously taken driving lessons, one should not drive metrics-based decision making without essential "data knowledge."

The COVID-19 pandemic and subsequent rapid valuation and devaluation of tech companies provides us with a recent example of what happens when such a fundamental understanding is not present: At the beginning of the pandemic, many online educational platforms, grocery delivery services, and collaboration tools saw a huge bump in new user sign-ups. Leaders at various levels within tech companies used these new figures to create projections. However, as soon as COVID-19 vaccination rates increased, those numbers returned closer to pre-pandemic levels. Yet many companies continued to use these recently gathered metrics and treated them as new standards, consequently unintentionally or intentionally creating false expectations both within their companies and outside.

2. Cult of Personality

Another common cause for weak ethical positions is the **cult of personality**. Environments in which the CEO of a company is set on a pedestal and treated as a god is one that encourages nepotism, and not critical product development. What counts is satisfying the leader, not developing a good product or creating value for the customer. Consequently, creativity and the freedom to do one's work are stifled, as those with decision-making capabilities seek to have their decisions validated by C-level management. That is, product decisions need to run up an entire chain of command until they are blessed by the cult's leader. In contrast, environments where this is not the case trust the capabilities of the individuals they hire, allowing them to make their own product decisions and execute on these. By placing one person above all, a company also inadvertently runs the risk of creating a culture of fear: the leader must be satisfied at all costs.

Leaders might initially believe in their product or goal, but once they lose themselves by focusing too much on either metrics or a personality, and not enough on building a good product, they have laid the way for a weak ethical position. Subordinates will follow.

Once a company has sustained a weak ethical position for some time, it will eventually become difficult to correct this position and change course. Shakespear's MacBeth captures the sentiment of many forced to work in companies with weak ethical positions: *"I am in blood / Stepped in so far that should I wade no more, / Returning were as tedious as go o'er"*

3. Words

There exists a fine line between marketing, self-delusion, and right-out lying, especially for companies that didn't find a Product Market Fit yet. When selling the latest technologies and trends, marketing specialists often try to use words that turn something inherently unhealthy, undesirable, or unethical into something that sounds healthy or "good." Just like marketers, we use words that avoid bad connotations throughout our workday in order to delude or trick ourselves into believing that what we are doing is right. In social media, a "flame war" is coined as "engagement." "Consumer engagement" and "weakening mental workload" really mean "forcing or tricking users into excessive/unnecessary consumption." When implementing analytics, we refer to "excessive data gathering" as "business intelligence." Other examples, and their translations, include

- **User retention:** Convince users to continue using your product when in fact they no longer derive value from it.

- **Stickiness:** Make it as difficult for a user as possible to stop using your product.

- **Virality:** A product that asks for friends' emails or contacts on social media in exchange for something on the platform, in fact spamming those that haven't shown interest in the product.

To avoid running the risk of a weak ethical position, leaders should therefore pay close attention to both product marketing and how their ideas are communicated in general.

The same can be said about marketing campaigns. Companies that rely heavily on marketing for growth often create artificial or inflated expectations to drive critical user behaviors or increase key metrics. Expressions like "Last minute sales," "Buy it while the stock lasts," or "There are only X spots left," for example, are leveraged loosely to incentivize consumption.

Unless they're authentic and evident, this attitude can have an external effect where consumers will gradually stop believing your brand and an internal impact that promotes the idea that this kind of misdirection is acceptable behavior.

If you find that your business is relying heavily on the aforementioned terms, then it may be time to examine the activities associated with them in more detail.

4. Market Incentives

Unfortunately, markets have a big impact on the ethical position of companies. And without the influence of third parties (i.e., regulators), the necessary forces to shape a baseline often do not exist. Let's take data protection and security for example. As Bruce Schneier aptly put it, "markets don't always reward good security." With the exception of some very specific industries—such as aviation or nuclear power plants—spending money on writing good, secure software does not increase the revenue of companies. Sony and Equifax are good recent examples of this. At Equifax, security and data protection seemed to be an afterthought, and even when security vulnerabilities were clearly evident, the company did not act on them (or acted on them extremely slowly).

Since writing good software is expensive, there is little that individual leaders at a company can do in this case. Instead, it is government regulation that can help make a difference. If governments would begin fining companies who fail to comply with industry best practices or ignore the safe-keeping of customer data, an incentive would exist for companies to invest money in developing good quality, safe software. As it stands, the market values bad practices. By forcing companies to pay millions in fines an artificial market incentive would be created that would favor companies with safe, good-quality software.

Although individuals in leadership positions cannot immediately influence what laws come into effect, they can help shape the future by collaborating with regulators and lobbying for political change.

5. Lack of Personal Identity and Accountability

Failing to hold people accountable creates an environment of impunity. Couple this with a lack of personal identity, and you have a recipe for disaster. This was the key finding from Zimbardo's Stanford Prison experiment, and one that we have seen repeated throughout history—from Nazi concentration camps or Abu Ghraib to holding cells and anonymous Internet forums. If you allow people to act as part of a mob without any sense of personal responsibility, chances are that they will do just that. Add other negative situational factors—such as propaganda, hate speech, risks to personal safety, tight deadlines, high stress levels, or high testosterone levels— into the mix, and people are likely to do and say things that they would otherwise never dream of doing. As Zimbardo more aptly put it:[4] *"allowing others to compromise their own responsibility, to diffuse it, makes them powerful backseat drivers and makes the car move recklessly ahead without a responsible driver. We become more resistant to undesirable social influence by always maintaining a sense of personal responsibility and by being willing to be held accountable for our actions."*

Note that "accountability" in this sense should not be confused with "blame." Leaders should never create an environment ripe with blame, in which heads roll on every occasion. Instead, they should build a collaborative climate, in which each team member can be the best that they can be. One in which the thoughts and ideas of individuals shine, and in which failures and successes are shared but are also *recognized*. Motivated individuals that are given autonomy and recognition tend to propel the product or team as a whole forward. And with this comes a natural sense of responsibility. A responsibility that is earned through ownership and achievements, and not imposed on by fear of blame, becomes difficult to diffuse as it wasn't the "corporation" that built a certain feature, but "you" the individual.

At the same time, leaders should avoid introducing de-individuating factors, such as online anonymity, uniforms, or the requirement for blind obedience to authority, and strive to protect the individual. Making people feel safe and accepted for who they are is the best and safest way to not only increase productivity, but to prevent the diffusion of personal identity and hence displacement of personal responsibility.

By not allowing the work environment to de-individuate the individual, and jointly promoting personal autonomy and responsibility, leaders remove the nourishment required by the "lucifer effect" to raise its ugly head.

Building a Strong Ethical Position

So far, we highlighted the impact that our environment has on our behavior, arguing that, in order to produce good actors, leaders need to create an environment that is conducive to good, ethical behavior. To this end, the previous section listed common factors that hinder the creation of such an environment—cult-like behavior, lack of personal responsibility, prioritizing numbers over quality, and so on. Eliminating such "negative" factors goes a long way toward building a strong, ethical foundation, but it is not the only

---

[4] "The Lucifer Effect: Understanding How Good People Turn Evil", Philip Zimbardo, ISBN-10: 0812974441

thing that needs to be done. Creating a strong ethical position requires leaders to look both *inward* and *outward*. The former means that they need to put policies and practices into place that shape the day-to-day behavior of individuals. That can involve

- **Requiring Software Engineers to adhere to the ACM/IEEE-CS Code of Ethics,**[5] which was published in 1997 and is an industry-standard code that aspires to promote the *"health, safety and welfare of the public"* and commits engineers to *"making the analysis, specification, design, development, testing and maintenance of software a beneficial and respected profession."*

- **Requiring employees to sign a company-wide Code of Ethics and Code of Conduct,** in order to ensure understanding of what ethical behavior entails and to guide individuals toward it.

- **Building Psychological Safety into the company's** culture which means creating *"a condition in which you feel (1) included, (2), safe to learn, (3) safe to contribute, and (4) safe to challenge the status quo—all without the fear of being embarrassed, marginalized, or punished in some way."* through team building exercises or building charters."[6] A common way to achieve this is through regular social events, team building exercises as well as developing charters.

No matter how safe workers feel, and how ethical they may act toward each other, a strong ethical position can never be achieved if the company's outward behavior is unethical. To that end, leaders should emphasize the building of products that help form a world that we want to live in, and this consequently entails paying attention to the company's mission and vision. In short, this notion can be summarized by the fact that we should not blindly follow cult personalities who proclaim that their software will change the world. Instead, maybe leaders should lower the tone a little. When CEOs speak to the public and proclaim that they "want to help the world," usually something big and impactful comes to mind. Unsurprisingly, those types of objectives are incredibly hard to achieve. A more attainable approach would be to aim for more realistic, achievable objectives. For example, customer satisfaction. By aiming for a high level of customer satisfaction (when engaged in legitimate business), customer satisfaction in itself becomes a proxy for "improving the world." Let's use Instacart—an online grocery delivery—as an example. At first sight, the product itself can be seen as a bit silly and the "time saved"

---

[5] https://ethics.acm.org/code-of-ethics/software-engineering-code/
[6] imothy R. Clark, 4 Stages of Psychological Safety

when it comes to grocery shopping is a "first world problem." However, imagine a couple that just had a child and both work full time. In that particular case, a tool that helps them deal with something so necessary as shopping, which can also be time-consuming, especially if you don't know the demands of a newborn, is a net positive to the world as it would save them time that could/would/will be spent raising that child. Framing problems and solutions in such "bite-sized"/niche forms, allows for a more realistic ethical baseline to be set. The alternative mission—"disrupting the industry" or "changing the way we live our lives"—means establishing unrealistic, far-away, megalomaniac objectives that are extremely difficult to accomplish and are either the shadow of a CEOs ego or the result of failing to understand the difference between a mission and a vision. While mission statements should be pragmatic and realistic, visions are inspirational. "Changing the way we live our lives" is therefore an acceptable vision, but not a good mission.

With realistic goals and mission statements set, leaders automatically counteract the causes of weak ethical positions. For example, the formation of a cult of personality is more difficult when the company's goals are not to change the world, but to move the needle on concrete items, such as customer satisfaction. Similarly, market incentives that encourage "bad behavior" on behalf of the company become less justifiable when you lower the tone of your objectives. Skimping money on data protection might be considered acceptable when you want to establish "world peace" (after all, leaking somebody's phone number is a small price to pay for eliminating so much suffering in the world), but it becomes much less justifiable if you simply aim to reduce the amount of time spent grocery shopping.

Of course, not all causes of weak ethical positions automatically become more difficult to assume through attainable objectives. Attainable objectives will, however, help you create a framework through which you can shape your operating environment. The goal of maximizing customer satisfaction, for example, allows you to establish metrics (such as first response time or NPR scores) that do not become an end in themselves, but instead feed into a bigger picture. Similarly, communication standards, or behavioral red lines, can be formed and justified more easily. Any type of communication or attitude that does not serve the concrete objective of, for example, maximizing customer satisfaction, becomes unacceptable. On the other hand, broad, generic objectives do not provide enough fire power. When "making the world a better place," a company as a whole gives itself too much leeway to prevent generally contentious internal communication. After all, the world would *not* be a better place without "free speech"—so why prohibit workers from sharing politically loaded messages?

At this point, we would like to emphasize that we do not want readers to confuse the previous sections with a moral crusade against business. We are indeed all in the money-making business. Just like you, and the vast majority of people, we want to earn money, or at least, care about becoming somewhat comfortably wealthy. However, the essence of this chapter is to emphasize the importance of making money by creating value for others. Not by misleading others or taking money because you feel "you deserve" it. There exists a difference between building a good product and manipulating users into spending money. Or—to once more quote *Francisco d'Anconia* (Ayn Rand's character from *Atlas Shrugged*):

> *When you accept money in payment for your effort, you do so only on the conviction that you will exchange it for the product of the effort of others. It is not the moochers or the looters who give value to money. Not an ocean of tears, not all the guns in the world can transform those pieces of paper in your wallet into the bread you will need to survive tomorrow. Those pieces of paper, which should have been gold, are a token of honor–your claim upon the energy of the men who produce. Your wallet is your statement of hope that somewhere in the world around you there are men who will not default on that moral principle which is the root of money. [...] Money is your means of survival. The verdict you pronounce upon the source of your livelihood is the verdict you pronounce upon your life. If the source is corrupt, you have damned your own existence. Did you get your money by fraud? By pandering to men's vices or men's stupidity? By catering to fools, in the hope of getting more than your ability deserves? By lowering your standards? By doing work you despise for purchasers you scorn? If so, then your money will not give you a moment's or a penny's worth of joy. Then all the things you buy will become, not a tribute to you, but a reproach; not an achievement, but a reminder of shame. Then you'll scream that money is evil. Evil, because it would not pinch-hit for your self-respect? Evil, because it would not let you enjoy your depravity? Is this the root of your hatred of money?*

In an ideal world, everybody would earn money by providing value; not by driving metrics or satisfying superiors. In the real world, we might not be able to adhere to this 100% of the time. However, at the very least, we owe customers a minimum standard of quality. Selling an ad-hoc solution that ignores security, best practices, and industry standards means you are neither true to your customers nor to your investors. If you are not true to them, why would your team be true to you?

Conclusion

In this chapter, we looked at the importance of building and maintaining a strong ethical position. In order to understand how to achieve this, we must know what undermines our ethical position. As such, we covered the five most common causes (based on our experience): (i) focusing too much on metrics, (ii) creating a cult of personality, (iii) the danger of marketing and bad communication, (iv) market incentives, and (v) lack of personality identity and responsibility. This was coupled with a discussion on the baseline (money) that drives business and how to ensure that you do not compromise it. If we were to summarize all of the above with one phrase, it would be this: earn money by building a good product (one that users *want*) with people that *want* to build it; not by forcing workers to manipulate customers into spending money. High ethical standards mean developing a solution to a problem that you can stand over together with people that accept the responsibility for building it.

Remote Work

As we've moved to virtual work, we haven't just coped, we've actually thrived. We are more focused on the things that have the greatest impact for our customers, associates and the business. We are making quicker decisions and acting. Meetings are now more inclusive of people regardless of location, level or other differences. We have great momentum and need to figure out how to carry it forward.

—Suresh Kumar, CTO at Walmart

We began working remotely long before the COVID-19 pandemic. That is, long before remote work became mainstream. Although remote work had already been a reality in the IT industry since the advent of the Internet, it had always been a fringe movement, primarily dominated by questionable "outsourcing" business models. Companies were usually operating a remote model in order to cut costs, and not in order to attract the best talent.

These remote workers were usually part of a larger on-premise organization: A model in which the majority of decisions were made in the office, while some members of the engineering team were remote. In short, we were the "guys working from home," operating in an environment whose hierarchy, communications, and day-to-day business were geared toward an in-person setting. The pandemic changed all of this drastically: Almost overnight, companies were forced to become "remote first," as opposed to "remote friendly." Consequently, every aspect of work changed—both from the engineer's and the manager's perspective. We will cover these changes in

© Benjamin Jakobus, Pedro Henrique Lobato Sena, Claudio Souza 2022
B. Jakobus et al., *Leadership Paradigms for Remote Agile Development*,
https://doi.org/10.1007/978-1-4842-8719-4_10

detail throughout this chapter, but in a nutshell, remote work amplifies the good and bad aspects of a company's culture and way of work. Specifically, our mode of working (remote vs in-office) affects how we communicate, collaborate, and trust each other, as well as how we balance our work lives and how we secure our data.

Communication

Communication is one of the building blocks of your business, and by switching into a remote setting, you automatically eliminate or limit the types of building blocks that you can use. Just like the type of material affects how much electric current can flow through it, the medium of communication affects your business' productivity, culture, and flow of information. By losing or reducing in-person contact and turning communication, asynchronous teams tend to become more productive as people's schedules become more flexible allowing them to work during hours in which their personal productivity peaks. Furthermore, employees do not lose time and energy commuting to work; they can spend more time with their families, make healthier food at home, and won't have their work interrupted by the noise and distractions that are a given in many office environments (the loud espresso machine, the noisy coworker, people walking past your desk, etc.). In other words, the remote worker, at least most of the time, has a much higher level of control over their environment. At the same time businesses save money: No offices means no rent or energy bills, no lunch or snack costs, and no cleaning staff or security guards.

While these are significant benefits, they come at the cost of narrowing the building blocks that you have available to build a good business. That is, there is no such thing as a free lunch, and you are paying for it by (i) making communication the most important pillar to your organization's success while (ii) at the same time making it much harder to implement effective communication successfully. An in-person team can get away with shoddy or ambiguous communication, as information flows through different channels—non-verbal cues, water-cooler chats, and so on. Therefore, a team is still likely to be able to execute (at least to some extent). The remote model however removes all other channels of communication and leaves you with a very narrow means for disseminating information.

In other words, by adopting a remote model, communication suddenly becomes the most important thing to execute correctly and, at the same time, the hardest. The reason for this difficulty lies in the mode of communication itself: Most remote communication is done by text, using chat tools such as Slack or Wickr. Consequently, this means that important aspects of verbal communication (such as intonation, gestures, facial expressions, eye contact, body movement, and posture) are either poorly translated or lost altogether. Once we lose their help, we realize that these "aspects" of communication are in fact resources that we rely on quite heavily. By not having those cues available to us, we are forced to craft a better message in order to avoid confusion or ambiguity. This, in turn, often requires more energy and attention—something that many people new to remote work often neglect. The unsurprising result is miscommunication.

Hanlon's Razor states: *"never attribute to malice that which is adequately explained by stupidity."* As can be seen in Figure 10-1, in the context of remote communication, a variant of this saying applies: *"never attribute to malice that which is adequately explained by miscommunication."* Put more simply: when we read a message from someone, we read it the way we want to read it and not necessarily the way in which it was intended to be read; furthermore, given the nature of written communication, we often have no way of telling how something was intended to sound. The safest, and most productive approach when reading a message is therefore to assume no bad intent. On the other hand, when writing a message, we should reject our urges to be short and direct. Yes, writing takes time, and on a busy day we often fall into the trap of assuming that being "to the point" seems like a good approach. However, it is important to keep in mind that we are dealing with people. Even if they appear like an abstraction to us that only lives on our screens, politeness and kindness are never wasted and help in making an already abstract environment more humane.

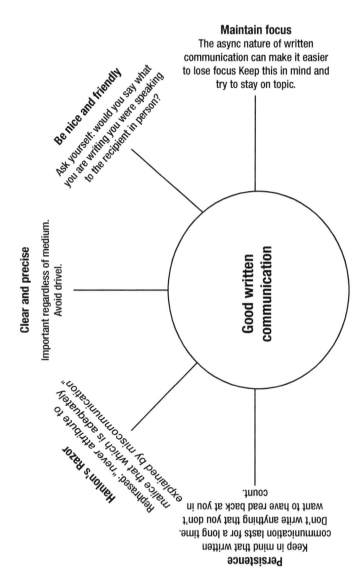

Maintain focus
The async nature of written communication can make it easier to lose focus Keep this in mind and try to stay on topic.

Be nice and friendly
Ask yourself: would you say what you are writing you were speaking to the recipient in person?

Clear and precise
Important regardless of medium. Avoid drivel.

Good written communication

Hanlon's Razor
Rephrased: "never attribute to malice that which is adequately explained by miscommunication".

Persistence
Keep in mind that written communication lasts for a long time. Don't write anything that you don't want to have read back at you in count.

Figure 10-1. The five elements of good written communication

Context

Our medium of communication also has a big impact on **context**. In verbal communication, a group tends to stick to a certain topic while different members of the group are discussing it. However, this is incredibly hard to achieve via text, as the very nature of textual communication is that it is asynchronous. As people exchange messages at different times, the innate priority brought about by verbal communication is absent for textual communications. To complicate things further, chat rooms are generic and persistent, which results in the tendency to reuse the same chat room for different subjects as most or part of the people we'd like to read certain messages are already present. This results in different topics being discussed at the same time and following and keeping track of what is going on much harder.

Last but not least, a part of your team may not be available during certain working hours— either because they are located in a different time zone or because simply they work different hours, and for that reason issues with communication cannot be clearly elucidated in a matter of minutes. For example, a task poorly specified to someone in a different time zone may need to wait until the next business day to get started because the message recipient was not able to understand what was needed. Combine that with time-sensitive tasks, and the demand for clear communication becomes evident.

While we painted a rather bleak picture of textual communication it should be noted that not everything related to textual communication is challenging. On the contrary: one very positive aspect of it is the fact that we can search for what was said in the past, making it easier to ensure everyone involved in the conversation is aligned. The issues mentioned above may also affect the searchability of a message but the simple fact we can go back in time and double check if we properly understood something is a feature not available in a verbal conversation.

Cultural and Behavioral Red Lines

The quickest and most effective way to prevent communication mishaps is to once again establish clear boundaries. Within the context of communication, that means clearly defining your company's culture and how you expect workers to behave, and to then draw very visible lines of what is and what isn't acceptable when on company time. One example of such a behavioral red line is the rule that subject matters should remain within the realms of what is professionally acceptable. This does not mean that colleagues cannot be friendly with one another or form friendships. Instead, it means that any topics that do not pertain to the core business of the company, or that risk damaging the company's culture/image and which have the potential to cause harm, injury, or outrage should be strictly prohibited. Companies that neglect professional standards when it comes to internal communication risk walking down a slippery path—a path that does not need to be traveled if clear cultural and behavioral red lines are established. Put more bluntly, "drawing behavioral red lines" means not allowing employees to share (using company's media or using the company's brand) propaganda or hate speech or any other content that might harm or needlessly offend others.

Oftentimes, once an *"anything goes"* approach to communication takes a foothold, it is difficult to root out. On one hand, contentious messages will upset workers. On the other hand, you risk creating a fanatical base that will cry wolf once you silence them. If you ignore one polarizing message, the employee that is being reprimanded for sharing another polarizing message will begin pointing fingers. The laissez-faire approach to communication in which one simply permits everything may sound tempting, but in reality will become extremely difficult to defend. As both a leader and a representative of a company, your first-most loyalty (during working hours) should be with your customers, product, and coworkers. That includes protecting and encouraging their psychological well-being and avoiding unnecessary conflicts. Depending on the culture of your company, the easiest, and most ethical, way to achieve this is to simply cut short any attempts at divulging and discussing polarizing topics. Simply do not allow it. Period. You are not founding a democracy. Instead, you are part of a professional organization whose mission is to execute, to produce a product or service. Within the context of your job, your ethical obligation resides with executing your responsibilities accurately and fairly, in a way that does not leave a trail of bodies behind. Remember: sometimes it's OK to be a bit authoritarian. Therefore, coming up with a clear, concise policy that anticipates this, and then sharing this policy with everybody before the problem happens, will save you headaches.

At this point, we hope readers don't jump to a conclusion that indicates that we do not value free speech. That is not the case, and the opposite is true (free speech is crucial and a fundamental right in our society). We are simply saying that, as a leader, you need to make sure that employees are happy and feel safe, and that as a consequence, workplace environments are not a natural or appropriate place for discussing all types of topics (that's what town halls, books, Reddit, pubs, family dinners, friends, political gatherings, or rallies are for).

Collaboration

It takes no genius to see that, in order to build great things, everybody must be in the same boat. A lack of collaboration between both individuals and teams means that unnecessary inefficiencies are introduced into the process of building your product. Instead of being able to focus on building the product, individuals will need to waste energy fighting with others. Good professionals will neither be able to give their best, nor will they be able to help others give theirs. This will inevitably all contribute to the creation of a toxic, high-churn work environment.

"Collaboration" trickles down from the top and is rooted in company culture. Uncooperative individuals in leadership positions will breed uncooperative teams below them. Fortunately and unfortunately, company culture can be difficult to change, and the feeling of "togetherness" and "belonging" is defined by the company culture as a whole. It is therefore crucial to get this right early on. A company that does not instill the importance of collaboration and belonging early on will find it difficult to do so later. In that sense, companies are like ships: the larger the ship, the more difficult it is to turn it around. A small motorboat can change course quickly. A large oil tanker will require a long time to turn around.

As companies adopt remote working models, how we collaborate with one another changes. While sitting alone in our homes, the feelings of "togetherness" and "belonging" can erode. Changes in the mode of communication may cause us to view or interpret colleagues differently, and an organization can quickly lose the human touch that an office brings. Suddenly, building a product can become more abstract, more clinical.

It is therefore crucial that leaders emphasize collaboration more than they normally might in an in-office setting, where the mere presence of like-minded colleagues can already instill a sense of purpose and meaning. Empathy, emotion, self-control, and regular video calls become increasingly important in order to help people remain grounded in reality. The more abstract our coworkers, the company mission, or the product becomes, the more difficult collaboration will be.

Trust

The importance of trust in an organization is self-evident, but just like communication, on a remote team, its importance is increased significantly. On the one hand, the employee needs to trust that the employer will pay him, of course, that seems obvious and certainly is not exclusive to remote work. However, imagine that the company is in the United States and the employee is in South America. Does this employee have any real chance of receiving his money if the employer refuses to pay? Could this employee spend the required time and money to access the US justice system? Would it be worth it?

On the other hand, the employer also needs to trust his employee more: Would the employer know for sure that this employee is allocating the time agreed by contract on the project?

It is no accident that platforms like Upwork, that mediate the relationship between employer and employee(or contractors if you will), have grown significantly,[1] as one of their main features is the responsibility that they assume on behalf of both parties (hence decreasing the need to trust each other).

Yet, according to our experience, companies and employees don't need to outsource trust. As illustrated in Figure 10-2, by maintaining the four elements of trust—openness, recognition, honesty, and autonomy—as well coupling them with some basic pragmatism, good communication, and some good will, the creation of an untrustworthy remote environment can be easily avoided (after all, employers simply want people to do their job; and workers execute their tasks in hope to get paid. As long as both of these expectations are met, and any bumps along the road get clearly communicated, trust becomes self-evident).

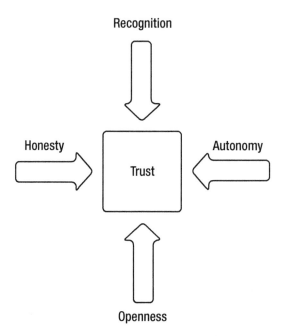

Figure 10-2. The four elements of good trust

[1] https://investors.upwork.com/static-files/3e32780b-95da-429b-9f36-22b5e508d6f7

With that said, let's take a closer look at the individual elements that help build a high-trust environment.

Info   Research shows that employees working in companies with high levels of trust experience 74% less stress; 106% more energy at work; 50% higher productivity; 13% fewer sick days; 76% more engagement; 29% more satisfaction with their lives; 40% less burnout.[2]

Honesty

Honesty is usually the first thing that comes to mind when we think about trust. It is also the most important. Without honesty, there is no trust. Period.

From the perspective of a leader, maintaining an honest environment requires acknowledging at least three key elements:

- Current problems facing the company (if you don't acknowledge them and your employees or coworkers do, then they won't believe you are able to address the issues)

- Expectations (be clear about what you expect from others and on which terms)

- Future (don't oversell what the company or team can achieve; don't cross the line between optimism and delusion; be realistic)

From a personal standpoint—regardless of whether one is leading or being led—it is important to understand the context and consequence of lies. Most of us tell lies not necessarily because we want to deceive the other person, but because it is easy. It is more comfortable to lie than to be direct and honest. We rarely consider the true impact that this has on our surroundings, however. In his book, *Lying*, Sam Harris highlights quite eloquently that it is not we—the liars—who get to decide whether a lie is big or small, innocent or not, but the people who we lie to, since *"people lie so that others will form beliefs that are not true. The more consequential the beliefs—that is, the more a person's well-being demands a correct understanding of the world or of other people' opinions—the more consequential the lie."*

---

[2]"The Neuroscience of Trust", by Paul J Zak, Harvard Business Review, https://hbr.org/2017/01/the-neuroscience-of-trust

So the next time you tell a lie—no matter how small—remember that the consequence of lying is that others will form beliefs and judgments based on the lies that you tell them. This results in a breakdown in trust, which results in collateral effects for which we all pay a heavy price. Once again, this is what Sam Harris means when he writes that *"I have never been burglarized, but I'm paying the price for people who commit burglary, through insurance and other costs."*

Recognition

Recognition plays an important role in trust as it highlights that the work being done was relevant and that the employee performed it well. Research shows that *"recognition has the largest effect on trust when it occurs immediately after a goal has been met, when it comes from peers, and when it's tangible, unexpected, personal, and public. Public recognition not only uses the power of the crowd to celebrate successes, but also inspires others to aim for excellence. And it gives top performers a forum for sharing best practices, so others can learn from them."*[3]

Autonomy

Trust is a two-way street, and autonomy is the best way to show people that you trust them. By giving someone autonomy over their work, you give them the freedom to execute their work to the best of their abilities. That is, you show that you trust the professional's expertise, creativity, and judgment.

Openness

Openness refers to the ability of a leader to share information with the team, as well as receive feedback. It is important to understand that many leaders confuse sharing information with relaying information. The latter simply involves forwarding knowledge that other people created. Sharing refers to making joint use of the knowledge. When a leader shares information openly they both relay, question, discuss, and apply information together with their coworkers, and are not afraid to show uncertainty or vulnerability. The latter implies asking for help, and is a very effective way to build trust as it demonstrates that one is able to recognize the limits of one's knowledge while also showing that one values the opinion of others.

---

[3] "The Neuroscience of Trust", by Paul J Zak, Harvard Business Review, https://hbr.org/2017/01/the-neuroscience-of-trust

Work-Life Balance

It is easy to see the benefits that remote work can have on our work-life balance. No commuting and complete choice to live wherever one would like, the ability to travel and see the world, homemade food, more free time/more time with family, better chances to lead a healthier lifestyle as well as a greater degree of overall flexibility are all invaluable advantages of remote work.

However, if we don't pay attention we can also fall victim to some problems that come with being far away from an office environment. For example, when working from home it is trivial to boot your laptop and start working but without proper discipline, it is also incredibly easy to

- Overextend the working hours – Extend a few hours of work because you are feeling especially productive.

- Work at unusual times – Can't sleep properly? Maybe you can advance some work for the next day.

- Check work-related content during leisure hours – Since I have my laptop here, maybe I should check some Slack messages or email to prepare for the next working day.

The above are only small examples of a whole range of behaviors that we can easily slip into if we are not conscious of them. By making them habits we run the risk of excessive stress or even burnout. Luckily, most of the negative aspects of working from home can be avoided by establishing a predetermined schedule that determines start and end times for work—just like we'd have in an office environment. Without such a fixed schedule, working from home can backfire and become a source of stress as it can lead us into the trap of assuming that we should be working anytime simply because we can. Remember: the fact that one can does not mean one should.

Data Security

Keeping data safe was always difficult, but it became a lot harder during the advent of the COVID pandemic, when remote work suddenly became mainstream. Sensitive data began leaving offices en masse, migrating into people's homes, and often leaving the hardware of the company to which this data belonged. At the same time, company workstations started connecting to office networks through unsecured media, exposing credentials and other sensitive information to whoever controls this communication medium. This coupled with a change in habit and behavior—such as the increased usage of company equipment for private purposes (leisure browsing, checking private email or social media) lead to an explosive mix of data breaches and cyberattacks. A recent study conducted by IBM and the Ponemon Institute[4] analyzed over 500 data breaches, across 17 industries and found that:

The average cost was $1.07 million higher in breaches where remote work was a factor in causing the breach, compared to those where remote work was not a factor. The percentage of companies where remote work was a factor in the breach was 17.5%. Additionally, organizations that had more than 50% of their workforce working remotely took 58 days longer to identify and contain breaches than those with 50% or less working remotely.

Such findings might not come as a surprise to many readers, and are not meant to discourage the adoption of a remote working environment. Indeed, many of the most security-conscious companies in the world today operate remotely, and have done so for a long time. There exist popular household names who are attractive targets due to the nature of their business, yet serve millions of customers without ever having suffered a data breach. What differentiates such companies from those that suffer breaches as a result of a change in work modality is in large part cultural: As opposed to being an afterthought, operational security is put ahead of everything else. That primarily means extensive and continuous training for employees on how to keep data secure, as well as sufficient overwatch by security professionals who ensure that best practices such as two-factor authentication, data encryption, and strong, one-time passwords are adhered to. In fact, organizations—whether remote or not—can avoid the *vast* majority of security problems via the latter. That is, by following six simple rules religiously:

1. Do not permit the use of work equipment for personal use. Ever

2. Only connect to office networks through a secure VPN

3. Enable and enforce 2FA on all systems

4. Enforce the use of strong, one-time passwords

5. Keep all software up to date

6. Continued education and awareness around scams/ phishing attacks

---

[4]"Cost of a Data Breach Report 2021" IBM Security,www.ibm.com/downloads/cas/ 0JDVQGRY

At this point, we want to emphasize that the above list is not exhaustive. We are not security experts, and entire books and university degrees have been dedicated to the topic of security alone. A company can follow our above recommendations to the T, and of course still fall victim to a wide range of attacks. However, following them should greatly diminish the risks brought about by the move from an in-office to a remote setting.

Conclusion

After working from home for a large portion of our joint careers, we arrived at a rather obvious conclusion: working from home rules! Its benefits are crystal clear: less wasted time and energy, more freedom and more control for workers, and reduced bills coupled with access to a much larger talent pool for companies. The COVID-19 pandemic has merely reinforced the model's feasibility. Nevertheless, leaders within companies of any stage and size must be conscious of the trade-offs that remote work brings with it. By being aware of how the home office affects how we communicate, collaborate, and trust each other, leaders can implement strategies that counteract any of the negative effects that are the direct result of the loss of personal contact. Furthermore, companies can mitigate the risks imposed by the potential loss of work-life and additional security threats.

A

Afterword

When we first set out to write this book, our goal was to compile a large list of common behaviors and practices that caused agile projects to fail—from faulty hiring processes to bad management. This list was rooted in shared frustrations, failed projects, and (what we perceived to be) difficult work environments. If we were to be perfectly honest with ourselves, we probably recorded these observations merely to air our grievances. But as we began analyzing and discussing our notes among ourselves, it quickly became evident to us that the true value in writing lies in the clarity that it provides the author. The process of sharing our collective experiences among ourselves helped us gain a deeper understanding of what it means to be a good leader, and helped us gain a deeper appreciation of just how complex dealing with people really is (both from the perspective of the leader and the led). Over time, and very slowly, this list of failures turned into a conversation. A conversation that we edited, tore apart, re-wrote, and refined. Over and over again, just like one would roll a snowball which eventually turns into a snowman. We uncovered new hidden debts to our past experiences—we saw how what we learned was not just shaped by the negative: indeed, the excellent colleagues, great bosses, and productive work environments were what helped us get to where we are today. As this book progressed, we tried to marry our experiences with the latest studies and theories in the field. We tried breaking down the problem of leadership just as a software engineer would break down a programming problem. Nevertheless, our book is far from perfect and far from all-encompassing. Just as no one shoe size fits all, no one book can teach you everything that there is to know about leadership or project management. There exist a vast myriad of different schools of thought, different leadership styles, and different management practices, and we have not even

B. Jakobus et al., *Leadership Paradigms for Remote Agile Development*,
https://doi.org/10.1007/978-1-4842-8719-4

come close to scratching the surface of what is an extremely complex topic. As such, we recommend that you, instead of considering our book as an authoritative guide, use what you have learned to gain an insight into what worked and did not work well when it came to our execution of remote agile projects. Remember the words of Arthur Schopenhauer when he wrote:[1] *"for the man who studies to gain insight, books and studies are merely rungs of the ladder on which he climbs to the summit of knowledge. As soon as a rung has raised him up one step, he leaves it behind. On the other hand, the many who study in order to fill their memory do not use the rungs of the ladder for climbing, but take them off and load themselves with them to take away, rejoicing at the increasing weight of the burden. They remain below forever, because they bear what should have bourne them."*

And with this, we bid you farewell, in hope that reading our short conversation was as useful to you, the reader, as it was to us writing it.

---

[1] Arthur Schopenhauer, The World as Will and Representation, Vol. 2.

I

Index

CPSIA information can be obtained
at www.ICGtesting.com
Printed in the USA
LVHW080415171222
735380LV00004B/304

9 781484 287187